Arunachala
Talks

Other books by Premananda
Papaji Amazing Grace

Forthcoming books by Premananda
Blueprints for Awakening
Songs of Silence
Arunachala Shiva

Forthcoming books by Open Sky Press
Face to Face with Ramana

Arunachala Talks

Spiritual Wisdom offered in a direct simple
expression to touch your Heart.

Premananda

OPEN SKY PRESS
www.openskypress.com

Arunachala Talks

Published by Open Sky Press Ltd.
483 Green Lanes, London N13 4BS
office@openskypress.com

First edition

© Open Sky Press Ltd. 2007

ISBN 978-0-9555730-2-6

Cover design by Devi
Cover painting by Premananda and painting p.55
Paintings from Darshana p.9, Ute p.31, Bhakti p.77, Shanti p.91,
Kali p.107, Saraswati p.141, Parvati p.167
Photographs by Chandi Devi ©2007 p.ix, back flap
Photographs from Sri Ramana Maharshi ashram p.viii, p.187, back flap
All other photographs from Open Sky House archive.

Printed in Hong Kong

OPEN SKY PRESS
www.openskypress.com

Acknowledgements

I would like to thank so many people who have contributed to the making of this book. They are so numerous that I am forced here to select just an essential few.

To my two direct Masters, Osho and Papaji, I owe an enormous debt of gratitude. Without my twenty years sitting at their feet this book could not exist. Ramana Maharshi came into my life quietly and invisibly, gradually becoming my main inspiration and guide.

My thanks to Kali Devi for her sensitive editing of transcriptions, accurately produced by Aruna from the meeting recordings. To Dakini, Darshana and Saraswati who, while translating this book into German, have made the final proof reading.

Thank you to Chandi Devi for the Papaji portrait and to Sri Ramana Ashram for the picture of Sri Ramana Maharshi. To Jyoti and Darshana who have taken the majority of the pictures from the Open Sky House archive.

Devi and Parvati for the graphic design and Shivananda for his invaluable graphic advice. Thank you to the Community residents who took part in the Arunachala painting event.

To all the residents of the Open Sky House Community for giving such loving energy support, creating a space for all those working actively on the book, and to Bhakti for feeding me late in the night.

Finally to Parvati, the director of Open Sky Press, whose painstakingly careful work has prepared this text for printing and who has given invaluable help in its preparation.

Premananda 2007

Oh, Arunachala, you root out
the ego of those who meditate
on you at heart.

Sri Ramana Maharshi

The pure Self is not realised
unless the mind subsides.
The mind is nothing but a bundle
of thoughts and the first
and foremost of all thoughts
is the primal 'I' thought.
Therefore only through the enquiry
'Who am I?' does the mind subside.
To keep the mind constantly
turned within and to abide thus
in the Self is alone Self-enquiry.

Sri Ramana Maharshi

Perfect Awakening
is possible here and now
for every human being, regardless
of background, practice or
personal circumstances.
You are already free!
Anything gained afresh will be lost.
What is eternal is always
within you, as your own Self.

Papaji

The surrender I am talking about
is a deep surrendering
to the moment and a deep
acceptance of what is.
Without any judgement!

Premananda

Contents

Introduction

Arunachala Talks consists of seven talks given to the forty-five participants in my annual Arunachala Retreat. The eighth talk was given in Europe on my return from India. This retreat, held in Tiruvannamalai, India, has been an annual event for the last six years. The message that is being communicated is the ancient Indian wisdom. I have nothing to contribute to that, it appears from emptiness and expresses through the body known as Premananda.

My contribution is in the communication of the message. I am a painter, a visual and creative person. I delight in the Arts. Music has a large space in my meetings and the community growing around me attracts creative people. So this book is unusual because great love has gone into its design. Hence the Community's photographs, graphic design and paintings are spread throughout this book, the colours reflecting the joy of the vehicle, my ecstasy.

I look at myself as a messenger for the teachings of my Master, H.W. L. Poonja. He saw himself as a channel for the teachings of his Master, Ramana Maharshi, the Sage of Arunachala. Arunachala is a holy mountain in South India. Ramana Maharshi spent his whole adult life on this mountain and considered it his Master.

The linage of Indian sages stretches back through Shankara to the ancient Indian wisdom which appears to be the core wisdom of most religions. Buddha walked the plains of North India and Jesus is reputed to have died in Kashmir.

Papaji's message was to 'Keep quiet' and from him I came to understand the great value of Self-enquiry, as proposed by Ramana Maharshi. 'Who am I?' and 'Be as you are', are the main components of the message I wish to share and are the essence of the talks in this book.

These eight talks discuss the main issues that need to be considered on the path to Awakening. *The Teaching of Ramana Maharshi* sets out how to follow Self-enquiry, which he considered the most direct route to Self-realisation. *Destiny* suggests that everything in our lives just happens, independent of our notion of 'doing our lives'. *The Spiritual Roadmap* gives an overview of the Spiritual journey.

In *The Fortress* I consider the ego or false Self, going into its origin and showing how it creates a filter that covers our True Nature. *Authentic Love* amplifies what was spoken in *The Self is Radiant*. Love simply is and you are that. I show how, for so many people, falling in love Hollywood style normally becomes the ultimate illusion, preventing Awakening.

Devotion examines the way of the Heart and shows how this is a necessary component in the search for Truth, more easily available in Asia than the West. *Presence* makes it clear that this is the simple Truth. When we are not in the past or future then we are present in the Now of this moment. The conditioned mind stops flowing and we are there in the vast power of Emptiness, which is our True Nature. In Truth, Peace and Love.

Premananda 2007

Foreword

Premananda was born in 1944 in Bangor, Wales, and grew up in Ipswich, a small farming town in England, 100 kilometres northeast of London. His family life as the eldest son with his parents, two brothers and sister was stable and loving, with plenty of space and encouragement for adventure and play. As a teenager he would have long conversations and debates with his father, far into the night, about the world, life and philosophy. Out of all that talking he was left with a very strong question that gradually increased during his early twenties but he had no idea what the answer might be. The question seemed to be about not knowing what to do with his life, not finding meaning in the world around him.

When he was nineteen, Premananda left the family and moved to London to study civil engineering, always with the strong feeling that he never really fitted in. He worked for a few years in a progressive design office with interesting people, specialising in building structures. However, he experienced sadness and confusion, desperately looking for the place where he would feel comfortable. Eventually he went back to university to study architecture. The curriculum was not only about architecture but included many other related subjects such as human civilization and culture. He graduated as an architect with a longing to explore himself and his relationship with life.

In his late twenties he worked as an architect and English teacher in Japan. He was also a post-graduate research student at Tokyo University studying Japanese architecture for three and a half years. On his arrival in Tokyo he experienced a huge culture shock and his internal question became even stronger. He went into a 'dark night of the soul' that lasted several years. He stayed on in Japan because he was engrossed in an internal dialogue that was provoked by being in that alien culture.

At twenty-eight Premananda still had no idea about spiritual life. While in Japan he met a German architecture professor who introduced him to his first master, Osho, although at the time he had no interest nor any idea of the significance of the meeting. Twelve months later, through a series of inexplicable events, he arrived at Osho's ashram in Pune, India. As he walked through the gate, which was called 'the gateless gate', he immediately felt at home.

Suddenly he had found his place. The feeling was emotional, powerful and strong and it was without any reason. It was as if the question he'd had for more than ten years was answered. For the next fifteen years he lived as an Osho sannyasin in India, America and England. Taking part in transformational workshops led to self-awareness and the years of meditation developed a quiet mind.

Two years after Osho's death, Premananda was living contentedly in Pune when he heard about another teacher, the great advaita Master Sri Harilal Poonja, known to his many devotees as Papaji. He read an interview with this man and also saw a video. But the real interest came when he started noticing people who had come back from visiting him. He saw an amazing transformation in these people. There was a glow and internal smile from them that touched him.

Although he had not been looking for another Master, he arrived in Lucknow and was surprised by Papaji's enormous availability. Osho had been the Grandmaster, but rather far away. Premananda found Papaji almost shockingly available. Shocking, because his immediacy confronted him with the question, 'Why am I here?' He had to really look and question, 'Who am I?' and 'What am I doing here?'

In the first three weeks, Premananda formally sat with Papaji in *Satsang* each day and three times asked him a question. On the occasion of the third meeting he saw with amazing clarity the thing that, during fifteen or twenty years of spiritual searching, he had never understood. The Self revealed Itself and it was seen that this was his True Nature, which had always been known. Without any doubt that meeting marked a total change in his life. Instantly the identification with Premananda and the story of Premananda were completely cut. From one moment to the next there was an enormous shift, which can only be described as an Awakening to the Self.

Premananda stayed on with his Master for five years. He continued to be part of the *Sangha* (community around a master) without any question arising. He ran the *Sangha* bookshop and hosted a guesthouse for visitors. Later he understood what a wonderful laboratory the guesthouse had been. Each guest brought an opportunity for him to see the structures of his mind. During this particularly creative period, he painted and exhibited his abstract paintings. He conducted the interviews for his book *Papaji Amazing Grace* and wrote poems.

At the end of the five years Premananda moved from Lucknow to Australia. Later, on the night Papaji left his body Premananda received a powerful energetic internal 'fax' message from Papaji telling him that he had some work to do. He was incredulous about this message even though the messages continued for two days. At the time he didn't know that Papaji had left his body. This was in 1997 and marked the beginning of Premananda offering *Satsang*.

At that time Premananda was living in Sydney. He had already collected a group of students for his meditation and reiki classes. He offered them an informal 'new' kind of meeting. The group expanded rapidly, a building was offered out of the blue and Premananda's *Satsang* life was on its way. For four years he offered regular meetings, weekends and retreats in and around Sydney as well as on visits to Melbourne and the Byron Bay area.

Since 2003 Premananda has been based in Germany and travelling widely in Europe wherever he is invited, illustrating the conditioned mind; the prison we build for ourselves from our identification with thoughts, emotions, beliefs, and desires. The demolition process begins as Premananda lovingly and humorously guides us to see that we are not the experience 'my life', but rather we are the awareness in which the experience happens. He focuses his meetings on this awareness, the Self, which is our True Nature and is revealed when the mind becomes quiet.

Premananda became associated with Ramana Maharshi five years before meeting Papaji. He found a hand-tinted photograph in a room he was renting in his last years with Osho. The beautiful eyes gradually made their way into his heart and being. Later he discovered this was Ramana Maharshi, whose teaching of Self-enquiry, 'Who am I?' and saintly presence had made him famous.

On meeting Papaji he was deeply affected to see that he had the same photograph on his wall. Premananda sees himself as a messenger for the ancient wisdom of India, the wisdom that forms the basis of most spiritual traditions. He is deeply grateful to his Masters for the understanding that allows him to share this message.

Premananda now lives between Cologne and Dusseldorf, Germany, in a residential *Satsang* and Arts Community of twenty people. The purpose of the Community is to create a fertile ground for Awakening. *Satsang* occurs in formal meetings and in the day-to-day life and forms the core of the Community. The most important part of the daily work is the work that happens inside each person. The work and working together create mirrors, giving constant reminders to look at what is happening inside. In traditional ashrams this is called karma yoga.

The Community is housed in a beautiful seventeenth century mansion, Open Sky House. There Premananda holds regular retreats and weekends. He has a closed *Sangha* group around him by his invitation, consisting of people who have a strong longing to become free. They meet with him on a regular basis. The Community is open to anybody who has come to the point in their life where they want to know themselves. Not their stories and dramas, but rather their True Nature. 'Who am I?' is the focus of the community and the motto is 'Be who you are'.

Premananda's first book *Papaji Amazing Grace* was published early in 2007. It is a collection of interviews with people who were with Papaji in Lucknow. It is Premananda's tribute to his Master, beautifully illustrating the love, devotion and grace that happen between devotee and Master. *Blueprints for Awakening*, interviews with Indian Masters, is his next book in which fifteen Indian Masters dialogue with Premananda about their teachings.

As an artist, Premananda has exhibited his paintings in India, Australia and Germany. They are in private collections in several countries. His joy-filled abstract paintings are an expression of the playfulness at the core of his being. He encourages and facilitates many forms of creativity at Open Sky House. Each week musicians are invited to perform for the public. Flow Fine Art Gallery exhibits paintings, sculpture and photography. Open Sky Summer Arts Festival is an annual six-day event of music, dance, theatre and art. The Community and visitors enjoy the use of dance and painting studios.

Premananda is no longer caught up in his conditioned mind, believing he is a somebody. Out of this emptiness, Self manifests as enormous energy and presence in each moment. Through his example Premananda shows us that spiritual life is every moment. It's not a special thing. *Satsang* is not special. There isn't really any spiritual life, there's just life. The whole effort is simply to be present for every moment of life.

Kali Devi 2007

A Spiritual Roadmap

Journey to Awakening

Satsang at the Rainbow Festival

Very often the spiritual journey
begins with a tragic event.
One day you lose your job,
you lose somebody who is dear
to you, or there is an illness or
accident and this event is a shock.
In this shock your mind stops, you
are present and you suddenly
have an Awakening.

Spiritual Roadmap

Journey to Awakening

Welcome to *Satsang*.

Very often the spiritual journey begins with a tragic event. One day you lose your job, you lose somebody who is dear to you, or there is an illness or accident and this event is a shock. In this shock your mind stops, you are present and you suddenly have an Awakening. In this moment the life that seemed to be going along day-by-day suddenly has no foundation. The ground where you were walking, which seemed to be solid, suddenly disappears.

The pain becomes unbearable and you start to look for help. Maybe you go to a bookshop, you try a meditation class or yoga class. Anyway, you start to really look at your life and this is a very important moment. In Papaji's words, 'In this moment you realise that you don't know.' This is actually very rare. Maybe one or two percent of the population come to this moment when they realise that 'I don't know'.

Everything gets a little vulnerable. You feel disturbed and so you start to reach out. If this longing to understand is really deep and sincere then in this moment a teacher appears who can help you to understand, and he will suggest some technique. If you carry out this technique the intense mental activity will begin to slow down. Then your mind will start to become peaceful. You will start to notice things changing in your external life. Things that brought you happiness will no longer seem so important. Along the way with this technique you will probably have some strong glimpses of stillness and peace.

If you have a good teacher he will confirm that this is your True Nature, that it is not such a big deal, and you should continue with your practice. After some time, it might be twenty or thirty years or it might be only a short time, your mind will become quiet and peaceful. Very few people come to this point.

If this longing is still true, and if it's still your priority, then the right teacher will appear who can guide you to Truth; maybe the same teacher, maybe another teacher. But you don't really look for this teacher. He will just appear in an unexpected way and you will immediately know it.

Then by staying in the *Sangha* (community) of this teacher, staying in the *Satsang* with this teacher, you may have even stronger experiences of your True Nature. Often you will spend the *Satsang* time in this True Nature but in your every-day life you will lose it. Of course, you can't really lose it because it is your True Nature. But the mental activity, the attachment to our story, our hypnosis with our boyfriend or girlfriend and our belief in the world out there, all conspire to put dust over this True Nature.

Nevertheless, at this time you can say your head is already in the lion's jaw. There is no going back because you know it doesn't work. Your relationships with your friends have started to change and the things that worked before start not to work anymore. There is no going back. You are firmly in the jaws of the lion.

Then suddenly one day, for no apparent reason, not because you've done something, there is a moment of 'Ah ha!' And in this moment, seemingly by Grace, you see with total conviction your True Nature. This is the moment of Self-realisation.

Everything changes and nothing changes. Life continues – before enlightenment, chop wood and carry water and after enlightenment, chop wood and carry water. But there is one big difference; there is no longer any 'somebody'. In this instant of 'Ah ha!' there is no longer this attachment to 'I'. We are no longer attached to 'my story', we are no longer attached to the world. At this point we might leave the teacher, with a lot of gratefulness, and go off to a quiet place and settle into this realisation. Or we may stay in the *Sangha* of the teacher. Either way, there is more work to do because in our psychology, maybe it is in our genes, there are certain tendencies. These structures of the mind (*vasanas*), or patterns of behaviour, are motivating our daily life and bringing much suffering.

These tendencies are like the rocks in a river. These rocks are preventing the easy flow of the river. In this moment of Freedom you are no longer really attached to these rocks. For example, one rock might be 'I am not good enough'. This strong belief motivates certain patterns of behaviour, in this case trying to prove to yourself that you are good enough.

As soon as you have this 'Ah ha!' you are no longer attached to the tendencies. So when a tendency such as 'I am not good enough' arises, it doesn't bite in the way it used to. It comes, you can have the Awareness of it, and if this Awareness is clear it can't bite and the tendency passes on. It will come again and again and it goes on and on coming. And just by watching it and not being attached to it, it will fade away. The river will flow a little more easily.

This is also my own experience. I came to Papaji after spending fifteen years with Osho. During those fifteen years I did many meditations and workshops and my mind became quiet. In fact, it became so quiet I thought I had come to the end of the journey. Existence even gave me a taste of being a guru. Suddenly, out of nowhere, I found myself travelling for six months in the Soviet Union with a wonderful caravan of people. It was about one year before the Soviet Union ended officially. In those days in the Soviet Union train tickets cost very little, also there was no employment and there was no food. It was a wonderful time. There was so much love and so many people came. Every weekend we ran a meditation workshop for fifty to a hundred people. The weekend cost five dollars and with this five dollars we were able to buy our train tickets and enough food for everybody. We would go to whichever town we were invited. It was totally unplanned, it just happened.

It was completely spontaneous. It took us from the Baltic Sea all the way to Tashkent in the east and then to the Black Sea in the south. We spent days on trains; there was this special energy and lots of miracles happened. Many people were touched and Premananda started to think he was a guru. But shortly after everything crashed because, of course, he wasn't really cooked. He was operating from the sixth *chakra* (energy centre). It's a beautiful place to live, it's very peaceful and you are apparently free. Many spiritual seekers stop their journey at this sixth *chakra*.

Existence picked me up and threw me down and I went through a difficult time. I ended up coming back to India, back to Osho, two years before he left his body, back to my peaceful life. After Osho had left his body, suddenly a new master appeared. I wasn't looking for one, I was happy with Osho even though he had died.

This master was Papaji. There was an instant recognition. At that time I had a wonderful girlfriend and somehow we managed to drive each other to the edge of the edge. We arrived in Papaji's *Satsang* and he was saying every day, 'Don't postpone! You can be free now. It only takes a few seconds. Don't postpone! There is nothing to do, in fact you are already free.' He was saying this every day and after three weeks I had this 'Ah ha!' It was an earth-shattering moment. It happened sitting in front of Papaji. There was no escape. It was the end of the road; there was some struggling and suddenly there was just whiteness.

Nothing worked. There were no thoughts; the eyes could not open; the body couldn't move; the body couldn't speak. Everything was white and very quiet, very still. After some time Papaji brought me back and had me sit next to him and there was an intense bonding or Oneness between us. Then there was a picture of Premananda spiralling into a huge void. It was very frightening and on the outside the body was twisting and going through strange behaviour. This was happening in front of the whole *Satsang*. Many people thought Premananda was mad, some people thought he was on drugs. But actually nothing was happening, there was a profound nothing.

I was helped to sit in the back of the *Satsang* and Papaji invited people to sing songs. Then he invited me back to the front. I could walk by this time. He told me, 'You don't have to come tomorrow,' but actually I did come tomorrow and I came for almost another five years. In these five years I never asked another question. I ran a guesthouse and every guest brought me some teaching. So I went through some intense processes and my rocks became very visible, sometimes quite difficult and yet not really difficult because there was a non-attachment to Premananda. The rocks melted slowly away and things became rather calm, still and easy.

Then after about four years there was a strong sense that I should leave. By this time there was a deep connection to Papaji; it was a bit like an internal fax machine. It was as if we could talk together without meeting and so for one year there was this big man with tattoos who was telling me, '*Chalo, chalo!*' which means, 'Go away, go away!' But I didn't want to leave. I was rather comfortable in my guesthouse. I didn't know were to go. I had been in India seven years. I had some fear about 'out there', and there was this intense love for Papaji; there seemed no reason to go.

It took one year and at the end of this year everything fell apart. The guests stopped coming to the guesthouse and nothing really worked. It was time to go. I sold off all the furniture and gave back the guesthouse. I had to decide if I would go to England, which is my home country, or go to Australia where I had never been before. Being a number seven on the *Enneagram* (a diagram of character fixation) I chose Australia. I like new experiences. I have already told the story, but the day after I left India I ended up in prison in Thailand, and there I discovered that I was always free. My inner freedom did not depend on my external situation. An important discovery!

In Australia my life started to develop not at all according to my idea, but in another way. I was teaching meditation and energy work and after two years I had collected some students. Papaji left his body and in that moment I got another fax message; it told me I had some work to do. Actually I didn't know he'd left his body at that moment. It was only two weeks later that somebody told me. I had been ready to deny this message, but when I heard that he had left his body exactly in this moment of the message I knew I couldn't escape it. I resisted for maybe six months and then I started these *Satsang* meetings.

It was very beautiful in the beginning; there was a kind of heat, a kind of fire. We started with six people and after only a few weeks we had about forty people coming to the meetings. Somebody had offered a building where we could have our own *Satsang* hall and it all came together very beautifully. And then Premananda noticed that his rocks were back. So *Satsang* would happen, a lot of fire and love, and then suddenly the next morning all the rocks would be back. Very uncomfortable. And then there was a feeling,

'I can't make these *Satsang* meetings because I have so many rocks!' I spoke to a friend who was also offering *Satsang* and he told me it had been the same for him; so I just relaxed. I can say now, after another five years, there aren't so many rocks left anymore.

Each moment is a new beginning. If you are willing to die to the last moment then the next moment is a new beginning and life unfolds. We can't know what the next moment will bring.

Question:
My problem is that I am not only thinking about myself but also about the people that I love and that are important to me. My story is the fear to lose the person I love, Sita. I think that I am not good enough so that she wouldn't have any reason to stay with me. I think she could meet someone else and fall in love with him and go away and say goodbye. This is a very old story; I thought it was gone but it's still there.

Did you enjoy Krishna playing with Sita in the bus? (The group had just returned from a four-day bus trip visiting five Indian Saints.)

No, not exactly enjoyed. I haven't come to the point where I can enjoy that. That is why I am sitting here (laughs)!

Would it be fair to say you have some attachment to Sita?

Yes, it's possible.

Well, the five Saints we visited had a clear message for you. What did they say?

Oh, my God that! Yes, I was more enjoying their Presence because I didn't understand so much.

They said that you should be *brahmacharya* (celibate). No boyfriends, no girlfriends, no sex. Don't even look at women. Don't lose your energy with a woman.

We have to look for a different guru! For India there is this kind of restriction but if there is an existing relationship it can go on, you can continue, it is possible.

Not if you want to stay with Thuli Baba (one of the Saints). You met this couple from Germany. Some years ago they created two beautiful daughters. They have been living with Thuli Baba for four or five years. They live in separate rooms and certainly for the last two years they've been celibate. If they were not celibate they couldn't be in that ashram.

Yes, that's their way. I haven't come that far. I am still attached to my stories and maybe that would be the easiest way to get out of them, but I don't want that!

What do you want? In the beginning of this retreat you told us that you came because you couldn't be seven weeks without Sita.

It could be possible. There is a switch, 'click', and then it becomes possible, but the question is if I want that.

My question is what do you want? Do you want a girlfriend or do you want Truth?

Can it be both?

Possibly, perhaps. Actually you are rather lucky with this particular girlfriend because this particular girlfriend is very interested in Truth. If you are both interested in Truth and both want to be together, and if you make Truth first and the other person second, then there's a wonderful possibility because your life together can be focused on Truth. You can support each other.

Shanti and Richard are in the same situation because they met in *Satsang* and they have a strong intention to be together. This can be based on Truth or it can be based on a love story. If you become focused on the love story, if it is important that the other person gives you love, then probably this story becomes very complicated. Most of your energy gets caught up in this story because unfortunately girlfriends are not like love taps. You can't just turn them on when you want love; it doesn't work like that. If you want something from them usually the story gets quite complicated, and in this complication you forget about Truth.

If you are focused inside yourself, if you know that you are whole and complete and you know that 'I am Love, nothing is missing, I don't need something', then it's quite different. Then you can simply play together, remind each other about what is important and stay out of the stories. This kind of relationship is rather rare. Most people's relationships are very energy consuming because they believe 'I am somebody' and 'I am loving somebody'. Two somebodies make a lot of stories. Because of this complication the traditional teachings suggest you don't have any boyfriend or girlfriend. In fact, Thuli said not even to look at a woman.

But he did look at women!

Yes, he is not talking about himself. In his ashram he only has young men, except for the Western people. You have to be really honest about what is happening inside and you have to really see your story with Sita. There is a sense that you do have some complicated stories and that you depend on something from Sita; she gives you something that you believe you are missing. Is that true?

I don't know. It is probably true.

You have to be very honest about it. When Krishna is playing with Sita is that relaxed? If it's not relaxed you have to be honest; why is it not relaxed? Is there a fear that this person who gives me love, which I need 'because I lack something', may go away with somebody else? Is that fear there?

There are many things. It's probably not just that.

Tell us what it is.

Yes, she could run away; why is it not me playing with her right now; if I back off, what does she feel then? I tried to completely get out of it, but then it's like a withdrawal or it becomes difficult because I don't know how to behave or what to do.

There's really only one thing to do, which is not really a doing, and that is to really connect to your True Nature. Then all your energy is focused inside, Truth becomes the most important thing and then you know you are whole and complete. You are Ram, so when Sita is there it's Ram and Sita. They are very nice together. When Sita is not there Ram is also very nice by himself.

Yes, if it's clear like that. But some situations are not so clear. For example when we are together but somehow we are not really together – then everything gets mixed up; that's really complicated.

The way to make it clear is never to be 'we' together. You always stand alone in the Self. I am the Self.

I haven't come that far. That's the problem and that's what causes the trouble. It would be very nice to just switch it off, throw it away. It would be really beautiful.

Yes, because then the play of Sita and Ram is more beautiful and it becomes so beautiful there's no chance of Sita running away. See? Sita will never run away when it's really beautiful. The whole of existence is Ram and Sita. There's nowhere for her to go. You remember I gave you these two names together? It's kind of a package deal.

I know.

So this play is very beautiful when it's free, when it's just happening by itself, when there's no story. And you know Krishna has a certain special meaning because Krishna goes with all the *gopies* (maidens around Krishna). So naturally Sita is also playing there. He has his own style. In fact all the girls are covered in bruises. This Krishna doesn't use a flute, and anyway Krishna already has a girlfriend. So he already has his own personal trouble. He doesn't really need any more trouble (laughter)!

Saraswati (a ten year old girl) likes to come and sit here next to me. But if I wanted her to sit here she would never come here. She would feel this wanting; she wouldn't find that attractive and she wouldn't come. When I first met her we had an instant meeting. I didn't really do anything and she didn't do anything. I said to her, 'Do you want to come on my scooter for today?' She said 'Yes,' so then I said, 'Well, we best go and ask your mum.' Mum said it was okay and we had a lovely day together.

It was really Authentic Love, the Love of the Self. Two months later you can see for yourself how, in the last two or three weeks, she has come here, has gone away from here, has gone to school, has gone to see her mother, and has come back here. She is choosing to sit here because of this love, but it's not loving Premananda. She also loves Kate, last night Kali was reading her bedtime stories and almost every person here has been sharing something with her. So what is going on? Actually nothing is going on! The thing that is beautiful about Saraswati is there is not 'somebody'.

There is really a Presence and this Presence is moving in the moment spontaneously. Remember when she asked Thuli Baba a question? This question was only possible because she absolutely understood what he was saying, and actually her question caught him. It was a very penetrating question but it wasn't really her question; if you like, it was everybody's question and her mouth opened. So in that way it was Saraswati's question. She is a wonderful teacher for us. She was attracted to this retreat. She has given everybody wonderful gifts, but you've seen she comes and goes. You can't put a contract on her love.

She doesn't belong to anybody, not even to her mother. Her mother understands that and is very happy for Saraswati to come here, very happy for her to be immersed in the love and stillness she finds here. So when Ram stays with Ram, when Ram makes Truth his first priority, Sita will never leave. She can't, because there is also then no Sita. For sure, if it is a love story between two people it will always have an ending.

Everybody has this *vasana* (tendency of the mind) of 'I am not good enough'. Everybody is exactly as God wanted them to be. So when you say to God, 'Well, God, I am not good enough!' this is very arrogant. There is something very beautiful in just accepting the way you are. This is a real surrender.

Question:

I feel eruptions of energy. I feel myself disagreeing with you, then I connect into my own inner light in silence. Stuff arises, but then it collapses back again and the light is still there. It's like a very, very high vibration in the light (laughter). I hear you talking about relationships and that they're just obstructions. Well, I know that and I know that even about my own relationship. I know what is going on there. But then I see your **Sangha,** *and it is really important for me to tell you that it will not stay dust-free and stories will arise. It is not different from an intimate relationship, even if you have five hundred single people in the* **Sangha** *there will also be blockages and bondages and borders and everything!*

That's right, but when you have one-on-one, one boyfriend and one girlfriend, there are two possibilities. You can find these Tibetan Buddhist statues where the Buddha is sitting with a naked woman in his lap. This is the dance of Shakti and Shiva. It's just light. There is total Freedom. This is one possibility and the other possibility is Hollywood-style love, and very often it's Hollywood. It is a very intense illusion. In the West it's necessary to confront this boy and girl illusion. People are hypnotised by it to the extent that the whole culture is directed at this illusion. The whole entertainment business of pop music, books and television soap operas is all directed at this Hollywood-style love story. People believe that if they can get this Hollywood love story right they will become happy.

Yes, I am not in that illusion anymore.

Yes, and it's still necessary to talk about it because many people, like Ram, are stuck in that story, and it's not the real story. The real story is to find the Self, to recognise that I am the Self and to ground in that, and then play. It's the only way to find happiness. You know this.

I know this.

So I don't need to talk to you about any of those things.

I have to say that even if my husband and I broke up it wouldn't be a disaster and even if the house burnt down – we are not so attached to that house, you know.

That topic was for your husband, not for you.

My issue is more that I'm taking on stuff for myself that's actually not mine; that's my tendency and then I get furious. The energy gets so strong and I am holding on and holding on and then I cannot hold it and it explodes. People are shocked and they think I am crazy or something like this.

You must look at why you screw on your own lid. You become like a pressure cooker. You don't have to light the gas because there is already a lot of energy, but you, for some reason, you screw on the lid and then the pressure builds up. It's beautiful that there is so much energy but you don't need this lid anymore. The lid of the pressure cooker has to be some old *vasana* and you can find out what it is. You can keep your awareness on it and when it comes into your life you know that you don't need to screw on the lid. You let it come because you can't stop it, because you know that it's not 'me'. 'Me' is the gas, the light.

Yes. My feeling is that I have always been in this space, this light, but I have always had the lid pushed on. When the life was smaller I could cover it, but now it is impossible because…

Too much light. You don't need the lid anymore. These old, wrong ideas don't fit anymore. Actually you have something authentic with your husband. I mean, we all know he is not perfect (laughter) but he is not so bad because he is here! He has come to India. He has come to this retreat. He sat on a bus for four days. This is lovely. He has a strong, busy lifestyle but he is not really in it. Osho used to say, 'Don't be of the world … be in the world but not of the world,' and this is his situation. He has this strong life but he is not lost in it. Actually you have something beautiful together because Truth is more important than the lifestyle. Both of you have your priority on the big thing. He is only impressed by Authentic Love. The Love of the Self. This is very beautiful.

It's about taking more responsibility about what there is and not just repressing it or giving it away. Just let it flow, whatever happens. I guess I could be very unpredictable then!

Great! Who cares about predictability?

I have to look for myself and from moment-to-moment really see what comes up in the light; no teacher can help me with that. I just have to see what's really inside of me and what the light says; if it differs from what you say, well, I have to see what's right for me.

Yes. For example I was listening to Thuli Baba talking about *brahmacharya*. In fact, I encouraged him to talk about it. Personally, I don't agree with him. As I see it the problem is not sex, but rather that energy is wasted by getting caught up in a story. I believe that you have to be very careful not to get caught up in Hollywood-style love stories. Sex is not the real issue.

I also asked him to talk about what technique he suggests for finding Truth. He said to keep the attention on God by repeating the name of God, saying, 'Jai Ram, Jai Ram.' It's okay, there is nothing wrong in it, but in my opinion Self-enquiry is much more strong and much more direct. I totally love Thuli Baba but I don't have to agree with everything he says; I don't make him wrong. I have my own path, my own journey, and out of this journey I have a certain idea of how to come to Truth. All I can do is to share that. Some people will be attracted and some not. But there's not a right or wrong.

My own expression.

Actually your paintings are like that. They're playful, in the moment, abstract. You are just expressing something inside in that moment. Your paintings are quite similar to mine, but also they look completely different. You use different materials and your fingerprint is different from my fingerprint. It's perfect. This is the beauty of life – that this same energy finds so many expressions.

My fear about this Sangha *is that there is no uniqueness possible. Everything becomes the same and everybody becomes the same and I notice that I behave like that in groups; I reduce myself to be like the others and I become boring sometimes. But that's me. I am like that.*

Yes, it's really your story because the whole intention about the *Sangha* it's not like that. In a way the *Sangha* isn't my business. It can go like this or it can go like that. It's not my business.

Yes, I have to look for myself.

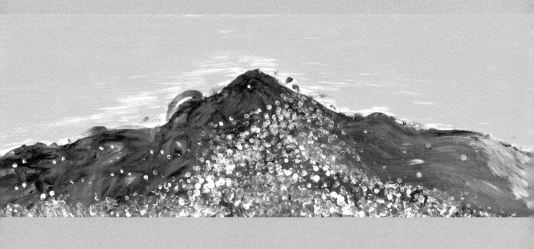

The Teachings of Ramana Maharshi

Who am I?

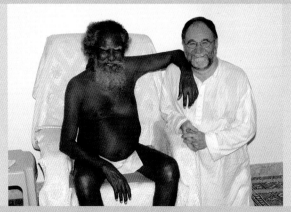

Meeting Sri Thuli Baba

The Source is constant. When
you keep coming to the Source
you always come to the same
place. It's you; it's the Real You.
When you deeply enquire with
this question, 'Who am I?' then
you find out that you are just
Beingness, just Pure Awareness.

The Teachings
of Ramana Maharshi

Who Am I?

Welcome to *Satsang*.

Everybody would like to be happy. All of humanity would like to be happy, but very often we don't feel very happy. We even feel unhappy. Sometimes we're a bit miserable and sad and when it gets worse than that we even feel a lot of pain. We need to understand what is going on. We have all been to *Satsang* meetings like this one many times and we know that the reason for our pain is our identification with the body and the mind. We are very identified with 'my story'. We deeply believe that 'I am somebody', 'I am somebody and you are somebody and they are somebody', and we experience this from the point of this somebody. This creates duality, it creates separation. Then the desire to be One comes up.

We all look for happiness and naturally we look for happiness outside. We buy an ice cream or some chocolates, a new dress, we look for a new boyfriend, a new girlfriend. There must be something out there that can make us happy and we constantly play this game. This is called desire. We have the idea that there is something we can bring to ourselves from out there and it will make us happy. It works in one way. If we are hot and sticky and we get an ice cream we feel quite happy, for a few minutes, with this cold ice cream. But very quickly it is not enough and then we buy a second ice cream which is a bit bigger and has more flavours. This bigger, better ice cream makes us feel good for a little bit longer, but it doesn't really work. So by the time you come to *Satsang* you've probably already eaten a lot of ice cream, you've probably had a lot of nice girlfriends and wonderful boyfriends, and you may have even bought a red sports car and the most fashionable clothes and still you don't feel particularly happy.

You begin to feel hopeless and life gets difficult, because how big an ice cream can you get? You start to feel exhausted from the effort to get a bigger ice cream. What to do? You feel hopeless and in this wonderful hopelessness you come to *Satsang*. Somebody there tells you that actually it was a totally wrong idea to try to buy a big ice cream because you were looking in the wrong place. This guy tells you that you have to look inside. That's okay. But then how to do it? What are you looking for?

Coming here to Arunachala, and to Ramana's ashram, we are as close as we could get to the answer to this question. Ramana Maharshi was suggesting a way of coming to your True Nature. When you come to this True Nature you find out that you are happiness. You find that actually there is nothing to do because your very nature is happiness, and even better than happiness you are, in fact, stillness and peace. This is better than happiness because with happiness comes unhappiness. When we take away all the thoughts and the emotions something is still present. It's very peaceful, it's very simple, it has no boundaries, it's very still, nothing moves. The Buddhists call it emptiness, no mind. In the Hindu tradition they call it *atman* (the Self). This Self is our True Nature. This Presence is your True Nature. So there is no question of getting something; you are this Presence.

There is one difficulty and this is that for many, many years we have been conditioned to always look outside. We completely believe in 'my story', and that the world and we are separate. We deeply believe this. It is a kind of hypnosis. It's so deep that even as I speak these words your mind is probably telling you that Premananda is a little bit crazy. It seems that if you want to come out of this game, out of this story, this story of me, then you need some help.

Ramana Maharshi suggested something he called Self-enquiry: to enquire about the nature of the Self, about your True Nature. Self-enquiry, he said, was the most direct method to know the Self. How to do this? What he suggested went like this: whatever you are doing, and it doesn't matter what you are doing, you can ask yourself, 'Who is doing this?' And the answer is 'Me.' Then you can ask yourself, 'Who is me?' There is no answer to this question. You can easily find some intellectual answers, but they don't help very much.

The effect of asking this question is it brings your attention from the outside to the inside, to the Source. If you continue to do this then your attention remains inside. In the beginning you can do this by sitting down with closed eyes and bringing all your attention to this practice. But after you've mastered this looking, or rather enquiring, as you pass through your day, no matter what you are doing externally, you can use it to bring your attention to the Source. The hypnosis, the attachment to the story outside, changes and you stay for longer periods at the Source. It doesn't really matter what you do on the outside because the whole effort is to come to the Source. The Source is constant. When you keep coming to the Source you always come to the same place. It's you; it's the Real You. When you deeply enquire with this question, 'Who am I?' then you find out that you are just Beingness, just Pure Awareness.

On a deeper level, the Truth is you are nothing. To be nothing sounds a little bit frightening but I know that being nothing is better than being so much! When you are so much, when you are 'the story', you bring huge baggage to each moment. So you can't really experience this moment. At least you can only experience it through many filters; these filters are, for example, your beliefs. If you are brought up in Japan you have one kind of belief filter, if you are brought up in Brazil you have another kind of belief filter. One is based on Buddhism, one is based on Catholicism. Then we have a certain kind of family, we might be the oldest child or we might be the youngest child, we might have very sweet loving parents or we might have rather tough and tyrannical parents. All this affects our filters. There are many aspects to this filtering and we have grown up to believe that we are all these filters: that's 'me'. The whole effort with Self-enquiry is to go much deeper than that. We want to find out what is in the very depth; what is our True Nature unaffected by all these filters.

When you look at the sky you see the clouds passing by. Are you these clouds or are you the blueness from which you perceive the clouds? Our True Nature is like the blue sky, it's vast, it has no boundaries, it's a constant, it doesn't change. When we are really there in this True Being there is no desire because we feel absolutely nourished. It's like being full of chocolate. When you are full of chocolate you have no desire to look for a piece of chocolate. It's a wonderful moment when you meet your True Nature. You discover there is no 'you'. So actually it's not a meeting – there is nobody to meet this True Nature – because you are the True Nature.

There are many ways to pacify the mind. There are breathing techniques, there are meditation techniques, there is chanting, you can say Krishna 50,000 times a day. One day here in India I went into an electronic shop and the owner was sitting at the cash desk. He was talking to me but he was always writing something. So I looked over the counter to see what he was doing. He was writing 'Ram'. He had books full of this 'Ram'. It was like a crazy homework. This man was writing the word 'Ram' hundreds of times, thousands of times each day. This is very beautiful because his attention was not on selling refrigerators, he was bringing his attention to God.

There are many kinds of techniques we can use to help us bring our mind first under control and then to stillness. These traditional practices have been passed down for hundreds of years. They help to bring the mind into a state of peace. This can support your life, it can make it more manageable and more enjoyable, but it is always duality. There is still somebody who is doing this meditation, somebody who is aware of the breathing. When people came to visit Ramana Maharshi and they didn't have any particular practice he would suggest Self-enquiry. If somebody came to him and they already had a practice, he would say, 'Very good, just continue it!' But he knew that at some point they would come to Self-enquiry.

We've travelled from many countries to come here to India. 'Wow, a whole new movie called India! How do I relate with India? How does India relate with me?' But this is the wrong question. You don't want to be caught up with this question about India because this means you are just replacing one story with a new story. 'In Germany the trees lose their leaves in the winter and now I come here and the trees are green, waving in the wind. How interesting!' But this is the wrong place to put your attention. The whole point is to come to the Source and that Source is the same in India and it's the same in Germany and it's the same in Australia.

My own experience is that travelling to different countries can be a benefit. It can help you to see that there is no point in being caught up in the story and it helps you to come back to the Source. Being together here in India there is an opportunity because everything is a little bit unfamiliar, even a bit strange, unusual. This can help you to break the hypnosis. 'I am English.' 'I am Japanese.' 'I am a man.' 'I am a woman.' 'I am a dentist.' 'I am a fireman.' 'I am a daddy.' 'I am a mummy.' 'I am a husband.' 'I am a wife.' 'I am a child.' Whatever it is, we want to let all that stuff go! It is very drastic when I say, 'Let it go!' I really mean let it all go! If you really want to know the Self, you have to let it all go! Not just the bad bits and keep the nice bits. You are just as attached to the nice bits as you are to the nasty bits. We are looking for something that is much deeper than that, more fundamental – the Eternal Self.

Question:
How can I let go of 'my story'?

You can let go of your story by continually coming back to the Source. All your different stories are connected to this idea of 'I'. This question, 'Who am I?' is a fundamental question. 'I am doing this and I am doing that'; these are the different stories – but it's always this character 'I'.

For me it's not always easy to come to the Source, because I have so many stories.

Right. It's very difficult to let go of the stories because you believe that you are the stories! So letting go of the stories is a little bit like death because you believe in this 'I'. We've all spent many years carefully constructing this 'I', brick by brick. We have constructed a fortress which is called 'my story'. What I am suggesting is that by using Self-enquiry you can start to question this story, 'my story'.

For example right now, if you look inside, can you find this 'I'?

Are you asking if this 'I' is really there?

Yes, where? Where is this 'I'?

This 'I' I experience as the I who talks, the I who sits here, the I who kind of everything...

That is what most people believe and this retreat is designed to question that; to ask if that's really the case. Is that really true?

So within myself there arises the thought that I can't really do anything. There is Grace and it just happens.

This is the point you see: am I doing this or does it just happen? For example if I raise up this arm is it 'I am raising the arm', or is it 'the arm is raising'? We have been conditioned to say 'I am raising the arm'. So everything we do we say, 'I am raising the arm.' 'I am talking.' 'I am drinking this water.' Yes? Is that true?

So there is no 'I'?

There is no 'I', but you have to investigate this for yourself. It is important that you really know this, not as an idea, not as belief, but as your experience, your knowing.

This is a paradox. Earlier you told us to put our ego in there, in the well, and then now you tell us there is no 'I'.

There is no ego. And there is no well!

There is nothing to put in there?

Nothing to put in there, there is nobody to put it in and there is no well.

Question:
A very practical question came up from this morning. When 'I', or whoever, woke up this morning it felt completely like I shouldn't stay in bed. I thought, 'Oh, I have to be the good guy and get up for yoga.'

Coming to a retreat like this is a certain kind of surrender, yes? You made a decision, or a decision has happened for some reason, to come thousands of miles on a plane to India and to come to this retreat. Something has pulled you here. Now you are here and you wake up in the morning and eight o'clock is yoga. You simply get up and go to yoga and you just surrender to that. If you are feeling 'I want to go to yoga' or you are feeling 'I don't want to go to yoga' or 'I don't feel to go to yoga' – these are all stories!

Up until that moment, when I woke up and thought, 'I should go to yoga,' there was no story.

There was no story until the story began, then there was a story.

I don't think there was a story that said, 'I don't want to go to yoga,' but there was no yoga until the moment the story began that I had to get up.

That's true, yes. There is no yoga until it begins, until you are part of it.

So if I stay in bed there simply is no yoga?

No, there is bed!

Okay, thank you!

The story is all the stuff that goes on in our minds: 'I'd like to go to yoga, it's very interesting, I've always wanted to do yoga.' Or 'Yes, I want to go yoga, but oh, that teacher I don't like him.' There are many stories, yes? Many stories are possible. This is all happening in the mind according to your beliefs and your particular conditioning.

Question:
What is the mind? Where does it come from?

What we are calling mind here is all our memories, all those experiences that we keep in the conditioned mind. We also have various expectations and fears about the future. All of this we call mind. In the moment when you are not in the past or the future, when you are just present, there is no mind. You can say the mind is peaceful.

If you are going to drive a car you will have to walk from here down the stairs. Your mind would guide your body. When you were young you were taught how to walk and how to go downstairs. Later you learned how to drive. All that information is kept in the mind, the functional mind. It is the personal mind, with its stories and memories from the past and fears of the future, which is attached to the 'I'. We are not really attached to the car being driven; this doesn't cause our unhappiness. It's the attachment to 'I am driving the car', 'I am raising my arm', the attachment to this 'I' that causes the unhappiness.

Question:
Does everybody have intuition?

What is this intuition?

Like a voice from the highest level of my being.

Well, the way you are speaking, the way you are probably thinking, the way you are expressing, is always that there is this somebody!

Yes.

I am saying there isn't any somebody and when you really are being – when there isn't somebody – then there is no higher or lower. It's just a flow. In our conversation there are several different stories operating and in one of the stories you are saying, 'This is my intuition, this is my higher self.'

So no matter what happens and what's going on I never have to decide anything?

How can you decide something when there isn't anybody to decide? You can only decide something if you believe there is somebody.

Yes!

But that's my whole point!

Question from a teenager:
I ask myself why I am here on Earth. I can say I am here because
I like to go to school, but this is not really it. Then I thought if I
don't find something then there is no sense in being here on Earth.
So then I can just be happy? What do you think?

This is a very good question. Why am I here? Why am I here on this earth? Why do I have a body? These are fundamental questions. These questions lead us to investigate about this 'I'. Amazingly you are here in this meeting and maybe you are the only person in your school who would come to such a meeting. Most of your friends are not interested in these questions – they are more interested in which pair of jeans they should buy.

I don't have any answer, at least I don't have any answer in the way of the world. We could say, 'I am here to eat as many ice creams as I can and then I will be happy.' I think many people believe in this answer, but this is not my answer. We are in a body and through our senses we experience the environment. We also have a certain consciousness with which we can understand that it's not about eating a lot of ice cream, it's not about the right shape of jeans.

So what is it really about? It can only be about knowing who we are. All our life experiences can bring us to the answer to this question. This is not an answer in the way of 'this shape of jeans is more fashionable than that shape of jeans'. When you really know who you are everything changes.

I think this is a very good answer (laughs).

If it is a very good answer it must come from a very good question. It's incredibly beautiful that you are sitting here asking this question. When I was fourteen I don't know what I was doing but I wasn't sitting in this kind of meeting! When you keep asking this question you will certainly get the answer. Once you get this answer, which you'll probably get when you are still very young, then your life will be very blessed. In a sense there is no death and so there is no real life. So then this question just disappears. We can say there is no point. There is no real reason, it's just like that; it's the working of Existence (laughs).

Question:
I experience the Self and the ego as a kind of weighing scale. If the contact to the Self is stronger the ego loses its weight and vice versa.

You could say that when my conditioned 'I', my ego, is not present the Self is present, and when the ego is present, when my strong sense of my personal 'I' is present, the Self is not present.

Very often it feels like floating, like changing from one side to the other.

Yes, we are all very conditioned by our personal story, by our ego. We are very attached to our ego. When you are in this attachment there is no recognition of the Self. In fact everything is the Self, so you are always the Self.

Yes, but sometimes the ego comes in front of the Self or something like that. It seems like Ramana lost this ego connection?

Yes. When he was sixteen years old there was a sudden Awakening and for some reason he had the ability to see that it wasn't 'I', it wasn't 'me', doing something. This is a very rare case and he became a great Saint. In fact it's so rare there is no point in being really concerned by that. If it's going to happen it will happen through the workings of God; Grace is perhaps a better word.

And because of this floating is it good to do Self-enquiry?

Yes, because what you are calling floating you could also say is like a transition. You are in transition from the person who just lives 'my story' to the person who lives in the Self. So the more this Self-enquiry happens, the more you will become rooted in the Self at the Source and less in the workings of the mind. Ramana said that you should do this Self-enquiry precisely and constantly until the moment of Self-realisation. There comes a moment of 'Aha' when it is absolutely clear and there is no more floating, you are no longer in transition.

I'd like to invite you all right now to see what your story is. It might be a terrible story, a very sad story, it might be a very happy story. Then you can ask yourself, 'To whom is this story happening?' The answer is 'Me.' And then ask yourself, 'Who is me?'

Question:
How can I handle this fear inside me, fear of transformation, fear of the death of the 'I'?

I think this fear is quite natural because when you are attached to the idea of this 'I', this somebody, 'my story', then naturally you would feel fear when faced with the idea of this whole story disappearing. Actually it is death and death means that somebody, the body and the mind, disappears. There is naturally fear about that. I think it is enough to be aware of it. You can also be aware that there are other times when there isn't any story and probably in those moments you feel very good; there is peacefulness and expansion.

In that moment, when there is nobody, you feel very good. This is an encouragement that death may not be what it seems. This is the death of something that doesn't exist. It's the death of an idea, a wrong idea, so it's not a real death; it's only the death of your wrong idea. When that idea is very strong it feels like death because you believe yourself to be all these stories.

It would maybe be nicer if it were easier.

I think naturally when you first meet this idea – that you are not really somebody, it's a little bit shocking and it takes some time to integrate and understand that.

Can you repeat that?

It's quite natural what you feel right now and maybe during yesterday's Self-enquiry session there were moments when there wasn't any story. You didn't really do anything, in fact by not doing something it happened. Actually there is nothing to do. There is a lot to do to maintain the story, but there is nothing to do to maintain you!

This also takes some time to understand because we have been so conditioned to do something to get something. The idea that by not doing anything you get it is a little bit difficult in the beginning. When you are simply being, things just happen. Last night I had agreed only to shave Ajay, then suddenly we had a hairdressing celebration! Things just happen.

I don't have to make any effort?

First of all there is nobody to make the effort. Is Premananda lifting his arm? Actually, the arm rises and then Premananda's mind says, 'I raised my arm.' Today I had a one-hour love affair. I was sitting in a cafe having breakfast, and I had a plan that I wanted to be very quiet, alone and read the newspaper. Okay, this was Premananda's story.

Suddenly a woman came and sat at the table opposite. We were looking directly at each other and she was very cute! She was either Korean or Japanese. I had a Japanese wife for ten years so I found her very beautiful. We started talking and she was very open and lovely. She came and sat with me and we had a wonderful meeting. It was totally sweet for both of us. Then we said goodbye. I also invited her to come and have dinner tomorrow night so you can all meet her and fall in love with her (laughter)!

She just spent three years in an ashram and her energy was very open. She was rather surprised by our meeting. This just happened and I enjoyed it for what it was; it was just that moment, about one hour. Then I got on my scooter and went to buy some distilled water. When I got to the town there was a parade with an elephant and lots of people carrying the gods around. It was a celebration. Then I enjoyed that. Of course there was no distilled water, but it didn't matter. Did Premananda do that or did that just happen?

It just happened (both laugh).

It's all just happening (laughter).

Ok, I'll just let myself be surprised.

You can just relax, it's wonderful!

Ok, I'll do that (laughter)!

Don't do it!

Why not, why not do it?

There is nothing to do!

Oh, yes, yes, exactly (laughter).

You can also enjoy being 'pissed off!'

My first thought when I came here was to say thank you for last night, because yesterday I had a horrible day and nearly everybody noticed that. Everything just dissolved in the moment when Premananda said: 'Okay, enjoy being pissed off for as long as it lasts.' This gave me the impression that it's also okay to be in this kind of state for some time. Nevertheless I have a question: how to handle this pissed off feeling? It's not that I don't notice what happens, I just don't have any means to do anything against it. I think I am aware of the fact but I just can't change anything.

What do you have to change? Who is deciding that you shouldn't be pissed off? Where does this idea come from that it is not okay? See that God gives us the possibility to also be pissed off, so why not use this facility some times? It's quite nice to be pissed off!

But it feels so tight, my whole body feels tight. How am I going to enjoy that?

Why do you have to enjoy it? Who said you have to enjoy everything? It's nice sometimes not to enjoy. Another possibility is that you simply surrender. What this means is you give up the personal doer. You give up the person who is going to change it from pissed off to very happy. You simply are the Awareness of pissed off and you are the Awareness of very happy. So you

51

don't have to do anything. Surrender means that you simply accept it as it is. As soon as you accept totally, it will immediately change because in that moment you are absolutely present. Okay, understand (laughter)?

My heart keeps beating very strongly. Since yesterday I feel this area, my chest and heart. I can feel what Ramana meant when he spoke about the Self coming out of this area. It's very strong. It's a kind of weight, pulling the mind. My heart is open again for Premananda, or better, for the Self. It feels much better than tight and closed. Can you tell me what Ramana says about the spiritual heart?

Yes, the physical heart is on the left side and Ramana says that in the moment when the mind really dies it goes back into the spiritual heart, which is on the right side of the chest.

But he says two fingers from the middle. In my experience it's right in the middle. What was your experience with this?

I don't have a strong experience with that. What he said is part of the traditional *vedantic* (non-dual system of Indian philosophy) wisdom in India. But as far as I know, it's a rare observation. What's more common is that the heart *chakra* (energy centre) is there in the middle and there is often a strong opening of the heart *chakra*. It's a significant moment because there are three *chakras* below and three *chakras* above. The three *chakras* below are to do with emotions and body functions and the three above are to do with spiritual aspects. When the heart opens it's opening towards the spiritual.

The spiritual teacher's first job is to help somebody open the heart. Out of this opening some spiritual wisdom is possible. For example the young Japanese woman I met this morning. I asked her about her three years in the ashram. She told me that sometimes it was very beautiful and peaceful and at other times it was a nightmare and she felt the teacher doing terrible things to her. But after three years she was completely open, like a beautiful rose flower. We could have this love affair because our hearts were open.

I've seen her three times already on the street.

Out of our meeting I have invited her here and it is meant to happen that she is brought to this *Satsang*. It just goes by itself. This heart opening is very important and until that heart opening has happened not so much else can happen.

Two days ago, when my heart was closed, I could feel it was almost impossible to get anything out of Satsang.

The heart opening is one period when it's very important that the seeker or disciple actually loves the teacher or the guru. The more intensely you love him, the more intensely this opening can happen. But it's not really personal; it's a device. The teacher is offering himself as a device to open the heart *chakra*.

In the last thirty years Osho Rajneesh did a wonderful job at opening the heart *chakra*. When you meet people connected to Osho they feel very much in their hearts. Since Osho left his body many of these people have moved to other teachers. Whatever the final decision would be about Osho's importance as a teacher, one great work he did was to open the hearts of thousands and thousands of people.

Presence

Here and Now

Sharing Presence

Presence is simple. Presence is
that which is when thought is
no longer there. Presence is also
Love, for when there is nothing
to block we are Love. Presence is
also Freedom because when mind
is quiet there is nothing to take us
away from this moment now. So
keep coming back to the Source
from which everything arises.

Presence

Here and Now

Welcome to *Satsang*.

There are two recent interesting spiritual books. One is *The Power of Now*, which became an international best seller, and the other is a series of three books called *The Power of the Presence*. So why use the word Power? And what exactly does it mean to be present? This is the crux of Freedom and it's so incredibly simple that it's almost impossible to get.

Presence is always now, exactly now, in this very moment; not in that last moment, not about what I had for dinner last night. It's not in the next moment, not about where we're going tomorrow. It's right now. It's when there are no thoughts of the past and no thoughts of the future; it's when there are no thoughts. There is a potential. Everything is functioning, consciousness is working, but the truth is, nothing is happening. The screen is blank. We can call that Pure Awareness.

In this Awareness there's the sound of a bird, the wind on the cheek, an Awareness of sitting on the chair and then another bird sings. We feel the warmth of the sun, hear the sound of the traffic and it's all happening Now. We're not evaluating it. We're not saying, 'Aah! That's a beautiful bird sound, but I don't like the sound of that traffic.' There's just an Awareness of Now and total acceptance of what is, without judgement. How can we know if it's good or bad? There is no active mind. Actually it's not quite true to say there is no mind. The mind is there as a potential. There's no story. Maybe a thought will come and then it will go. It doesn't disturb the Presence. It's just like that.

Why use this word Power about Presence? When you're really present nothing can shake it. I remember once sitting with U.G. Krishnamurthi. He's about eighty-six now, and he's a well-known anarchistic spiritual teacher and an interesting man to meet. He's rather small. He travels with a small bag. He eats porridge twice a day. He looks about seventy and his energy is more like fifty. We were on the top level of a hotel in Sydney and suddenly somebody turned on a pump on the roof.

It was very close and noisy. He didn't miss a beat; it was wonderful talking to this man. We were supposed to be having a discussion, but in the end he spoke non-stop for two hours and occasionally I said, 'yes', a few times 'no', and if I was lucky I could squeeze in a question. He would put something forward. He would talk about it and then he would close it up. It felt as if he put down a stepping stone and invited me to stand on it, then he put down another stepping stone and just as I was standing on it he would take up the one behind. At the end of the talk it was like nothing had happened. Nothing was left and there was total Presence, vibrant and powerful. This small man eating porridge twice a day, he is a personification of Power. Not in the sense of executive power. It's like sitting in front of a cool tornado. Very focused.

There's nothing to do to be present because it simply is. It's absolutely a given. In fact, you have to do something not to be present. You even have to do a lot. As soon as you stop being caught up in your mind you are absolutely and automatically present. You are free of any baggage and old stories. You live on the edge, with no idea what the next moment will bring. Everything is a risk, and you don't care. There isn't anybody to care. There's just an Awareness, we can say a Pure Awareness. Living in Presence is a wonderful way to live and it's the whole attainment of spirituality.

Let's just close our eyes for a moment. Feel your feet on the ground. Feel the weight of your body on the chair, the slight coolness of the air on your skin. Hear the sounds - children's voices, birds singing, the traffic, some voices. Some thought passes. The sound of the birds seems to be a little louder. Perhaps there is some pain in the body. The wind ruffles the hair. Traffic passes by. Something opens inside. An emptiness, expanding, seemingly without boundaries. The odd thought passes. Sound of the traffic. Wind on the cheek. Bird song. Traffic sounds. Bird song. Often what happens now is that some thoughts arise and suddenly we identify with those thoughts. Those thoughts lead to other thoughts. The whole story starts. We no longer hear the sound of the birds because suddenly we're absolutely in the story.

We're feeling terrible. We're remembering last year's holiday. It was a terrible holiday. It rained every day and the food was awful. There were so many mosquitoes and the traffic was terrible, awful pollution, the room was uncomfortable, had no view at all and I fell out with my girlfriend. It was just the most terrible holiday.

You become absolutely attached to this movie, the movie of last year's holiday. You even start to get emotional about it. It seems to be absolutely real as if it's happening right now, but in fact it's just a memory. You become totally attached to it. There's no sense of Presence. You don't hear the traffic. You don't notice the wind on your cheek. You just remember the mosquitoes, the rain and breaking up with your girlfriend. It was a terrible holiday.

That's the way we lose Presence because we become attached to our mind, to some thoughts or stories mostly from the past. But they can also be from the future. Sometimes we have tremendous fear about the future. This fear takes over our daily life. We have no idea how we can get from here to there. 'How can I pay the rent? How could I buy that train ticket? How will I survive?' We become transfixed by this fear.

It is 'somebody' who is afraid and it is 'somebody' who is not going to survive. It was 'my' holiday, 'somebody's' holiday. I completely lose touch with Pure Awareness. These attachments are always a wrong identification. We're always getting identified again with 'somebody'. When we are present there isn't anybody. There is Pure Awareness, an empty screen on which everything impinges.

Become aware of your body: your feet on the ground, your spine against the back of the chair, the breeze on your skin. Become aware of the sounds: the traffic, the birds – a kind of symphony. Perhaps a thought is passing by. Not much is happening. There is a certain space, a sense of peace, stillness.

Being present is like being in the flow of the river; moving without effort. Things just seem to happen. In exactly the right moment the right person appears: 'Oh, you're going on a bus tour and you have a DVD player in the bus. Go and see Gabriel he has many DVDs.' There's no effort to Presence. But it takes tremendous effort not to be present, 'doing' my life. Just flowing down with the river with no effort, things unfold spontaneously. And when you become attached to a story, in that moment you can rescue yourself. You can ask yourself, 'Who is attached to last year's holiday? I am attached, and who is this "I"?' When you do this enquiry it takes the energy away from the story and back to the Source. The Source is this Presence, it is this Pure Awareness, it is the Self, the Eternal Self.

The other day you met Hans, a German man. He took you up onto Arunachala. Thirty years ago he met Papaji in Switzerland. He was attending the lectures of J. Krishnamurthi, the famous teacher. Every year he gave a series of lectures in Switzerland. He would speak every other day and on the alternate days Papaji would be available. On one of those days, Hans met Papaji. He was very impressed by that meeting because he noticed that Papaji seemed to be very present most of the time and he realised that was what he wanted. So he became very connected to Papaji and some years later he would spend up to three months at a time in India, even sharing a room with him. One day he said to Papaji, 'Your experiences of Presence seem to be much longer than mine,' and Papaji answered, 'That's not the right way to look at it. Presence is not an experience. Presence is your nature. "Your life" is an experience.'

We've become so conditioned. What we think of as normal and natural actually requires great energy. It takes a lot of effort to keep all these stories going. Papaji was pointing to something very important. With the understanding that these stories are not important we can just live in this Presence, in this Pure Awareness, with nothing in between. Anything that has happened is already garbage. It has already passed. The whole effort is just to be present, yet it needs no effort. Actually it needs an absence of effort. This is your nature, so it is very easy. You don't have to understand anything. You don't have to do anything. It's just a given.

I remember one time in India I was sitting with Satchitanand in his room. He is the head of a large ashram and many people were coming and meeting him. Just before, I had made a donation. I put some money in an envelope and he gave it to his assistant who put it in the drawer where he was sitting. Satchitanand went on with his meetings giving spiritual answers to some people, and then one of his assistants came in with the electricity bill. He stopped what he was doing. He just glanced at the electricity bill. Perhaps he was checking the total to see how it compared to last month's bill and then he nodded to his assistant, gave him the bill and pointed to the drawer. Then the assistant opened the drawer to take the money for the bill but there wasn't quite enough money. Then he opened up my envelope and there was exactly the right amount of money that was needed. The assistant left with the money and Satchitanand just continued his meetings. Almost nothing happened, and in this way he was running this big ashram.

It doesn't matter what is happening on the outside. If you're really present there's Pure Awareness. It doesn't matter if there is Pure Awareness of the electricity bill or Pure Awareness of a spiritual conversation. The Awareness is the same. Presence is the same.

Ramana Maharshi was famous for sitting on a couch, but he also liked working in the kitchen. Each morning he got up very early and went to the kitchen. He prepared the breakfast for the ashram and he helped to prepare the lunch. We don't hear much about that because that was not really for the public. The visitors who came to the ashram met him on the couch, they probably weren't there at four o'clock in the morning when he was in the kitchen. For him it didn't matter if he was sitting on the couch or if he was chopping vegetables. The same for you, it really doesn't matter what you do. If you're present, you're present. You can be present with a vegetable or you can be present with somebody coming to meet you.

Spiritual life is every moment. It's not a special thing. It's not that this *Satsang* meeting is special. The whole effort is simply to be present for each moment of our lives. In a way you can say there isn't any spiritual life. It's just life. As the Zen people say, 'Before enlightenment, chop wood and carry water and after enlightenment, chop wood and carry water.'

In the next few days we are going to meet five extraordinary spiritual Masters. In India they are called Saints but you'll find they're very ordinary, very simple. What they have in common with each other is Presence, and you'll feel the Power of that.

When we visit Thuli Baba, you'll see that people are in the habit of bringing biscuits and sweets to his *Satsangs*. His assistant prepares them all on a tray and then at the end of the *Satsang* Thuli takes the tray to each person and gives some biscuits. But he does it in such a way that it's almost like he's giving you the most delicious chocolate, even though it's just an old Indian biscuit. He is very dark skinned and almost naked, just wearing a little loincloth. He has a very big belly but he walks like a king. You can enjoy the Presence because being in his Presence you'll find it much easier to be in your Presence. A kind of magic happens.

These five men are not going to give us a great philosophy. They will probably tell us nothing that we don't already know, but you will feel that your life has changed. It's like you've seen a beautiful sunrise in Antarctica over the purple colour of the snow. It's something rare you've never experienced before and your life becomes enhanced, touched, and yet it was just an old, ordinary biscuit. Nothing special, but you felt something because maybe in that moment you became really present. This moment of Presence changes your whole life.

Question:
Everything flashes away so quickly. When I go back in my memory I think I've already experienced moments where everything started to glow, but then I'm tricked out of it very easily.

So what happens in this trick?

These 'nows' go by so quickly. Yesterday the reason I didn't sit on the couch was because I felt I could only talk about things that were already over.

What isn't flashing by? What is constant?

The perception of me being it or not being it. It changes.

Is there something that doesn't change?

Contemplation. Watching what happens.

And who is the watcher?

Somebody who's judging, having an idea of what the watcher is supposed to look like. My body gives me a hard time and this is difficult for me.

Maybe you can use these changes of your body. If you put in some chemicals the body has one kind of feeling about it and then, after some time, another. It feels different, but there's something that doesn't change.

The only thing that doesn't change is the watching.

What's there when you don't try, when you don't have any judgements and when the body is changing?

Awareness. I used to be much less aware. I decided that I just owe it to everybody else to be as present as possible so I can give whatever is possible.

That sounds like a lot of effort.

Sometimes I think I'll just give what's there, as it is, without manipulation. I also play a little bit with it because I don't want to be anything special.

Sounds like a lot of effort. Why don't you just be you? Just totally accept yourself without any judgements and without any idea about how you should behave.

Okay.

The beautiful thing about life is that you're completely allowed. God is just asking you to do your dance. You can learn from Saraswati (a ten year old girl). She's dancing with God. See, you never know what's going to happen but from this dance we feel, 'Oh! This is Saraswati's dance,' and somebody else is dancing in a completely different way.

I would like to love everybody.

Why would you like to love everybody? Is that better than hating everybody?

I would like to live in the Awareness of everybody dancing.

Live in the Awareness of your own dance. The particular form of dance isn't important. If you look around you will see each dance is unique, and the more authentic and unique the dance is the more we notice it and the more we love it.

We all know that the lion is the king of the jungle. You never hear about a sheep being the king. Your dance is just as unique as anybody else's dance and this Awareness that I'm talking about, this Presence, is absolutely the same for everybody; only the dance is different. For example, we're going to meet these five Saints. Their saintliness is the same, but each one will be expressing that quite differently.

The sentence I like best is, 'There are no non-spiritual beings.' It's nearly the same as the thing you just said about there not being any more or less spiritual things to do.

I was really trying to say that everything is spiritual. Life itself is spiritual.

So why are we trying to make it special?

Well, we're not. You're trying to make it special. I'm not trying to do anything.

When I look around I see churches, temples and other religious institutions, but for my own part I'm responsible for myself and it's like that for everyone.

You see, when you speak in that way you're continuing this whole game of somebody. You're totally caught up in the stories. The invitation is to see that you can live in a very simple way without maintaining the correct presentation of your story to the world, and without making a judgement about each thing. You can simply accept the stories as they are. Everybody has many stories and some of them are very tragic. Every family has the drama of birth and death, and this we can call life. It's just like that. When we can accept this the whole quality of each moment of life changes.

I'm also not very fond of the story.

Yes, but you don't have to judge that: that you're fond of it or you're not fond of it. This is your life. When God was shuffling the cards you got that card. Some people are blind. Saraswati has a sister with brain damage. Maybe you met her yesterday. She has very good intelligence but her body is a bit of a mess.

You said everybody is Presence. It is not possible not to be Presence because it is our nature. So even when there appear to be stories there is still Presence.

When you become identified with a story you are no longer in this Awareness.

Yes. I am more likely to be caught up in the event.

You become identified, don't you? You become attached to this event, to this thought, and it consumes you so that there's only the story and there's no Awareness. You become absolutely identified and you believe that this story is real. Right now you know that nothing is happening, but I've experienced many times that you're absolutely in the story and then you're experiencing that a lot is happening. Maybe later you can say nothing happened because in Truth nothing did happen.

My question was not so much about stories but more about the meaning of Presence, because even when there appear to be stories there is still Presence.

When Mount Everest is covered by a cloud Mount Everest is still there, but you can't see it anymore. When there's a big story you can't see Mount Everest. Presence is always there because you are Presence. There is no way it could not be there. But when there is a strong story and you become attached to that story then you are identified with the story and no longer identified with Mount Everest.

Everybody is a Mount Everest.

But what happens is you become identified with the clouds covering Mount Everest. You believe you are the clouds.

Yes, but Mount Everest is always aware of itself.

This is the whole point, it's not aware of itself. It becomes aware of only the story, the clouds. If you become identified with the clouds, the story, you have no Awareness of the True Nature.

Question:
Then my mind comes in and says, 'Well, this is only a trick. You don't want to stay in this story.' When I'm in a story it helps to step back and do Self-enquiry and ask who is it being caught up in the story. Just now when you were speaking I was in a black story. I said to myself, 'Well, that's nice. Let's step back. Who is it?' Then I had the feeling, 'Oh well, this is only a trick to get rid of bad feelings…'

It's great! Self-enquiry a wonderful trick, if you want to call it a trick. But there's nobody to say it's a wonderful trick. Just use it and as you use it more and more you will discover that you are this Mount Everest. Then when stories, clouds, come you don't get identified. It doesn't matter if it's a black story or a white story. You can just blow away the cloud around Mount Everest and you see again that you are Mount Everest. This is the whole teaching of Ramana Maharshi. When you're in this black story you're just caught in the black story; but if you can remember to use this trick, something changes. It changes very quickly because it's very hard to stay with the story when you see Mount Everest, knowing that you are Mount Everest.

The point is I couldn't use it in the right way... I didn't get out of this cloud. So for me it's not the point to get out of it, but to accept it and to love it.

Tell us again what happened when you did this Self-enquiry.

I just had bad feelings and I thought I wanted to express them and let them out, like we did in the therapy groups in Osho's ashram in Pune. When I stepped back from these feelings the thought came, 'You have to go through it again and it's not allowed. This is only a trick. You have to stay in it, otherwise it's not real.'

But these clouds aren't real. You know that because if you just totally accept the cloud it will change very quickly. It's not real. No story is real. We're trying to find out what is real and I'm suggesting that the thing that's real is Pure Awareness.

Don't identify with the cloud. The point is to use that trick to take you out of the story back to the Source of the story. It prevents you being totally identified with the outside, with the apparent world, with the mind and all the different stories arising in the mind. We want to bring all that back to our beingness. It's a wonderful trick!

I was asking for the process of this trick but I have to find it out on my own.

No. I can tell you. There's a big black story and you've been totally in the story for some time. Then there's an Awareness of this story and then you ask, 'Who is experiencing this black story?' The answer is 'Me.' Then you say, 'Who is this me?' This second question brings you back to the Source. It reminds you immediately that you are Mount Everest and it breaks the identification with the cloud, with the black story. When you do this constantly it's much, much harder to get identified with stories. We get easily identified with the stories because our whole conditioning has made us believe that we are all these stories. This is a wrong idea and the Osho therapy way doesn't help very much. It perhaps makes the stories less black, but here we're trying to do something much more fundamental. We have to break that conditioning.

We don't really care if it's a grey story, a white story or a black story. It may be easier to live with a grey story so the therapy helps in that way, but we're trying to see here that we're not the story. We're simply Pure Awareness. We simply want to live present, in this moment. When there is some big black story the Presence is still there, because that's your very nature, but in that moment you have no Awareness of the Presence. You're simply identified with the black story. After a couple of encounter groups the story becomes a grey story then a pinky-white story but it's still a story. That's one of the things that's a little bit sad about therapy and the Osho ashram. People go on and on with the latest therapy groups and their stories go from black to dark grey to lighter grey, then a bit white, and a bit pinky-white. Years go by in this way and nobody ever tells them that they're not the story. I have some wonderful friends who go every year to the Osho ashram. They have been visiting for twenty-five years and nobody got it that they're not the story. The colour of the story doesn't make much difference.

Nobody wants to run away from a wonderful story.

Yesterday I talked about relationships, about falling in love. Definitely a good story! During the honeymoon part this is the ultimate illusion because the story is so sweet you can get addicted to it; but it's still a story.

Question:
I want to share something. Twice last night I was dreaming an unpleasant story. All of a sudden I realised I was dreaming and then I stopped the movie and I woke up. It was okay.

Yes, we often have these horrible nightmares and just when a knife is going to strike us we wake up because it's so shocking. We find we're just in bed. There's no knife. There's relief, 'Phew! Wow! Great!' and this is the whole effort of *Satsang*.

Yes, that's what I thought because in daily life it's the same.

It's the same thing. I remember when I was first told that the waking life and the dreaming life were not much different. I thought, 'Rubbish! How can you say that? That's nonsense.' But this is the whole point of *Satsang*. When people first come to *Satsang* it sounds like complete nonsense. We don't want to be told that we're asleep. 'How can my life be just an illusion, like a dream? My life is very important. I love my boyfriend.' The whole effort is to wake up and to see that all this stuff is our conditioning and has a similar quality to our dreaming. We're very resistant to this.

It's a great relief to just realise the story.

Maybe it's not such a relief when your story is good. Perhaps you're dreaming that you're in a bath full of champagne and when you wake up you're just in the bed!

That's what bad stories are good for, to wake up!

Yes, in one way. It's harder to wake up from good stories. In some ways it's helpful to have a black story because when the story is very painful you can't bear to be in the story. Then you have to really look and there is more reason to do this trick. But when your life is just champagne it's easy to stay in that, and many *Osho sannyasins* (disciples of Osho) do exactly that. They've been doing therapy for many years so they've changed most of their black stories into pinky-white stories and they've done many years of meditation so their minds have become very quiet, very peaceful. They've created a lovely lifestyle and their egos are very happy because they're part of a special club of spiritual people. They know they had the best Master because he had piles of Rolls Royces, he looked really good and there were many beautiful people around. So they stay on this peaceful plateau. This wonderful Master even talked about it. He called it the sixth *chakra* (energy centre) plateau and he warned these same people to be careful of it. I can remember also living very happily in this sixth *chakra* plateau. In those days my journey seemed to be finished. It's a lovely comfortable plateau, a nice lifestyle, but it's not woken up and it's not Free.

The Self is Radiant

The Self and the Mind

Celebrating the Moment

We are not separate, and at the
same time each mind-body is
absolutely unique. We're simply
invited here for a short time to
sing our song. You can simply say
thank you, be very grateful and
enjoy the play.

The Self is Radiant

The Self and the Mind

Welcome to *Satsang*.

The Self is radiant. The Eternal Self is like a shining diamond. The Self is subtle. The Self is stillness, peacefulness. Nothing moves. Emptiness. With no boundaries. A constant. Never changing. The mind arises from the Self. The world manifests from the mind. When the world is there, the Self is not there. When the Self is there, the world is not there.

We go to bed at night and in the beginning we have a light sleep and sometimes dreams are there. These dreams are like thoughts. There's not so much difference between the thoughts in the waking state and the dreams in the sleeping state. Then we go into a deeper sleep and in that deep sleep there are no dreams. This is the Self. So everyday we spend maybe six or seven hours in the Self. In this deep sleep there's no world. The mind-body organism is functioning, but there are no thoughts. When we wake up in the morning we feel a deep sense of nourishment. This time in the Self nourishes us.

We're ready for the new day. There's a small moment between opening the eyes and when the mind starts being very active; it's an opportunity. When you first open your eyes the mind is not busy because just one moment before you were sleeping and now the eyes are open and nothing has happened. The mind is very still and in that moment the Self is present. So if you wake up with a great Awareness, you can just simply wake up in the Self. When you bring more Awareness to this you can expand that space of the Self before the mind becomes busy, becomes activated.

We've looked at this small booklet from Ramana Maharshi, *Who am I?* and he says very clearly that when the world is present then the Awareness of the Self will not be there, and when the world is not present the Awareness of the Self is present. Yesterday in this long *Satsang*, the Original Face, as time went by you noticed that everything became quieter and quieter in the room and everybody was affected by that stillness. All the minds became quiet and by the end of the six hours there was a tremendous stillness. Several people experienced a wonderful peacefulness. There is a quality that is not possible if the mind is very active.

How to still the mind? There are many different techniques. You can meditate, do breathing exercises, say *mantras* (sacred sounds), you can even constantly repeat the name of God. All these techniques will still the mind but, unfortunately, the stillness depends on the technique. When you stop meditating or you stop the *mantra* then the thoughts come back. How to still the mind in a way that the mind doesn't reappear, that the mind doesn't bite?

Ramana Maharshi suggests there's Self-enqiry. He says this is the most direct way to Self-realisation. When you enquire into your own activities with the question, 'Who is doing this?' the answer which immediately arises is 'me'. Then when you ask yourself, 'Who am I? Who is this me?' there's no actual answer. But the effect of asking this question is to bring your attention from the outside to the inside. It brings your attention to the Source and there at the Source rises the mind and from the mind, the world. So when you constantly do this Self-enquiry your very strong attachment to the world out there becomes weaker. Your attention starts to come inside more easily and rests in this Source. At the Source nothing happens.

It's very still and, as you experienced yesterday, this stillness feels very peaceful. You recognise it as something very familiar, very close, because this is your True Nature. There's nothing to do. The mind would always like to do something. You don't have to do anything! In fact, any doing is taking us away from our True Nature. As we come into this non-doing we lose interest in the stories. We lose interest in our own story and we lose interest in the other person's story. We lose interest in the story of the world. Everything falls away and as it falls away we don't want to go anywhere, we don't want to do anything because we understand that the Self is complete. Nothing is missing. There's no desire because desire comes from the idea that I am missing something. 'If I had that then I would be complete.' Desire is always making us move to the outside. There's nothing to get. It can't be any better because right now it's complete. The Self is complete.

Once you come to see that 'I am the Self' you don't want to go somewhere and you don't want to do something. Right here is enough! Of course you may go somewhere, the body may move, the mind and body may respond to something. It might suddenly start raining and you move to a dry place, or if you're cold you move to the warmth. There's no better and there's no worse. So life becomes a kind of play, *leela* (divine play). Things happen, the body moves, the mind is active, but all the time I know I am the Self; I am whole and complete. Nothing is missing. There's a deep relaxation. All our striving and struggling finishes. The beauty of Arunachala is that it seems to make the statement that this is the place. Stop here! As if it's the end of the road. Here we can stop and everything is taken care of.

This morning, just outside the meditation room, there was a beautiful black bird sitting on a wire. Last year he was also sitting there and the year before as well. That little bird really likes that piece of wire and so he's just playing there. Every morning he sings his song for no reason at all. When you stop for a moment and look in a big mirror you find out everything is wonderful. In fact, you're exactly as you are meant to be. Just like that little bird sitting on the wire. When you look around at the other mind-bodies in this circle everybody is unique. There aren't two the same. Even the identical twins are not so identical.

This existence is so abundant, each one unique, each one a perfect manifestation of God. We just have to accept it and stop the war, stop this constant desire to be different, to be somebody, to say to God, 'I'm sorry God, but actually I don't like the way you made me. You should have made me a little bit fatter or a little bit thinner.' What is happening in this retreat is not that we're all trying to become perfect. Perfectly like who? The beauty of this group is that each one is unique but the energy that comes through, the Self that illuminates each mind and body, is the same Self. So we are not separate. We are absolutely the same, the same One. At the same time each mind and body is absolutely unique. So we're simply invited here for a short time to sing our song. You can simply say thank you, be very grateful and enjoy the play.

This is the beauty of having this retreat in India. We're so close to celebration. Wherever we go in the street there is a celebration of the moment and this makes us feel more alive. In the West things have become a little bit serious. We have a strong sense that we have to do something. We're very busy. We have no time and here in India there seems to always be time because the moment is important and we can feel that. Somehow this opens us up and we love India, but it's not really India. We love this feeling of aliveness. There's a space inside and we're encouraged to celebrate each moment.

Question:
You say that when the Self is there the world is not there. What exactly do you mean by this? Do all objects disappear?

No, the objects don't disappear, but the force of the objects changes. The attention is on the Self and not on the objects. The world doesn't disappear. For example, I see the world in the same way that you see the world, but my attention is here, at the Self.

So you see the pictures, but you are not attached to them? No story about it?

Yes. There's no story about it in the way that I might say, 'Oh, I hate the rain. It's so wet today.' But if it's raining I put up my umbrella.

And why?

There's no reason. Our friend Hans, he puts up an umbrella when the sun shines. This is his play.

Okay, so we can say it takes the seriousness out of it?

In the sense that it takes away this serious response to the objective world, that it's real.

So it's like living in a cinema movie and enjoying the pictures?

It's not really enjoying them or not enjoying them. It's just like that.

All the time?

All the time. When you're established in the Self then it's all the time. Doesn't matter what the play is outside. I remember a friend of mine in Lucknow talking about what had happened to him. He had an Awakening and his life changed. In those days Lucknow was a very polluted city and he told me that even when he sat on his scooter behind a big truck, everything was wonderful. In that kind of acceptance, that kind of play, the quality of life changes because things become very simple. When you're not choosing and when you're not judging and when there's no need to do something then life becomes very simple.

Saraswati, our ten year old, interrupts to ask:
Is it like you see it there but there's nothing to do about it, just let it be?

Yes. Remember John Lennon's song with the Beatles, *Let It Be?* I think he learned that when he went to Rishikesh with the Maharishi. As soon as you have a big investment in changing the world then you've got a big job because you're basically saying, 'Well God, you didn't do it quite right and so I need to change it.' Then you're very busy for your whole life. People often feel uncomfortable if I say that the world is okay the way it is. They say, 'Well, what about the beggars? What about all the sick people? The starving people? You know, what about the wars? What about Hitler? What about all these nasty things that happen?' I say, 'Well, this is the play of existence. This is the play of God.' They want to change it. They want to make everything nice.

When you're in the Self do you only see the good things and never count the bad things? For example, you only count all the good things about the beggars on the street?

You don't make any judgements. You don't judge what is good and what is bad. It's just like that.

It's there so why don't you let it be? You can't do anything about it.

Yes, just let it be.

Question:
Something happened two days ago. I experienced that the 'I' dissolved and what is left is the body, the mind and the consciousness. I'm wondering how it is possible that the 'I' creates itself out of these things again and again. Because actually there is no 'I', but it really feels like there is.

But isn't it more like a shadow of an 'I'? Like an empty skin, you know, like there's no guts to it?

Well, this sense of 'I' is very familiar to me, so it's very easy that it reinforces itself every moment, especially if I'm walking, doing and speaking (laughs).

There's a very strong momentum. As you say, it's constantly reinforcing itself.

Two days ago this Fortress Satsang really helped me to get a taste of the ego. Before, I always had this sense of 'Wow! That's the way I am,' but to really taste this ego structure is horrible.

Yes, we've constructed for ourselves a beautiful gilded cage – our own prison. Once you get a taste of that then everything starts to change. Ninety-nine percent of human beings never come to see that. They live from their birth till their death completely in the story, completely believing it, with no idea that there could be some other way to live. When you really get a sense of the fortress then something changes.

It's a really strong illusion, but there's still this sense of 'I' even in the middle of the consciousness. Maybe it's more this kind of 'I am'. Yesterday I got upset because there was so much filming and then I asked myself, 'Who is disturbed?' Then it was gone. It's really, really amazing working with Self-enquiry.

This simple remembering of 'Who am I?' is so strong.

Yes, and I can use it everywhere, every time.

Yes. Ramana Maharshi was asked if you should do this all the time. His advice was to do it constantly, until the moment of Self-realisation. The mind is so programmed. We've been experiencing everything from this 'I' for our whole lives – every moment for thirty, forty, fifty years; but Self-enquiry can constantly bring us back from that. In the beginning it's not so easy to come inside, to come back, because our attachment to the objects and our belief in the movie of the world are so strong. As you do Self-enquiry the attachment becomes weaker and this huge investment in the world gets to be less and less.

Out of this I can see the importance of a retreat or staying with a Master for longer periods.

Yes, this is a wonderful opportunity. Choosing to come here with a group of people who want the same practice and who support each other is a wonderful moment in your life. In the regular daily life in a busy Western town there are strong structures. There are family and work. We are busy fitting ourselves into society. It's much more difficult to come to the Source but it's not necessary to leave the world. You don't have to go to the Himalayas to a cave for twenty years, but you need to make your own cave – to be in the world, but not of the world. We've become conditioned to believe that if we are in the world we have to be of the world, but it's not true. I've lived now for about thirty years in the world but not of the world. This makes me a strange kind of person. People can feel that I don't really fit in.

I think that's what is meant by priority – our Awakening has to be the first priority.

Yes, this is absolutely needed. If you don't make it your first priority you have no hope. If something else is your first priority then naturally that puts you in all the structures of society, the world, the family and so on. Then you're in the world and of the world you will never meet the Self. This is very important to understand; people have the idea, 'Oh yes, it's my first priority,' but it's not. For example Daniela, a musician. About five minutes after she first met me she was telling me, 'Oh, Premananda I know you're going to be my guru.' She's been with quite a few different teachers but meeting me was very particular for her. We held two very nice *Satsangs* in her place and then she came to the Inner *Sangha* (community around a master). This is a group of people who want to make Truth their first priority. We meet four times a year for very intensive weekends. That first weekend she was very positive and she had all kinds of ideas.

Then she sent a big email telling me that she's leaving the *Sangha* because she can't afford the time to come to the meetings. Four weekends a year is too much time for her. She's busy with her work and her family. So I don't really know how to respond to her now because for me it doesn't add up. If she won't even give four weekends a year to be totally focused on Truth, what's the point? She actually understands a lot of things, but she doesn't live it.

If you want to achieve something it has to be your first priority.

The Fortress

The False Self, the Ego

Enjoying the Play

If we could get to this one stone
– the foundation stone – the rest
of the fortress could fall down very
easily. Self-enquiry brings you to this
foundation stone. Instead of taking
the fortress down brick by brick
there's a possibility of the whole
thing collapsing in one moment.

The Fortress

The False Self, the Ego.

Welcome to *Satsang*.

We've asked ourselves the question 'Who am I?' and today I would like to go a little more deeply into this question of the 'I'. Most of us have now got a clear sense that there is something we could call the big 'I', which I call the Self or the Eternal Self. The word 'eternal' is indicating that this Self never changes. It never changes in the infinity of time. Bodies are coming and bodies are going, for an instant; the Self remains. *Satsang* is suggesting that we are this Self and that we are not the body nor the mind. When I say mind I'm including the mental thoughts and the emotions. Both of these are mind. When we look inside and say 'I' we generally don't mean the Eternal Self. We mean my story. 'My story' we can call the identification with 'I'. This is also called the ego, and I'm using the image of a fortress.

Recently I went to a beautiful retreat centre in Germany near Bremen. The owner of this retreat centre and his young wife had a ten-day old baby. We were sitting very quietly in *Satsang* one evening when he came in with this baby wrapped up against his heart and simply sat down quietly. Nothing was said and after some time he left with the baby. There was an amazing sense of God entering and God leaving. I could sense it in the silent space.

When this baby entered there was a feeling of everything opening up, a kind of expansion, and equally when the baby left there was something like a slight contraction.

Of course, I'm talking about something very subtle. Although the baby was no longer in the mother's body it would have no sense of separation. For the baby it would not be so different and the parents were very sensitive and kept the baby wrapped up and close to their bodies much of the time. But at some point that baby will get bigger, as babies do, and start to crawl around. One day she will stand up and a bit later she will start to talk and, somewhere in that process, she will recognise and say 'Mummy'. A bit later she will say 'Daddy', and then probably 'baby' or, if baby has a name, 'Shakti'.

From that beginning a sense of separation develops, because there's baby and you. Let's say John and Kate, so we are two. That creates the beginning of separation even though energetically we may still be very close. The baby may still feel totally one with the mother and everything else; the world is a little bit hazy, not so clear, not so defined, but gradually things get more set. At some point some toys are offered and then maybe a little friend comes to play. The little friend starts to play with the toys. He picks up one of the toys belonging to John and John grabs it back and says, 'MINE!' because by now John is totally identified with the toys and thinks they're part of him.

He experiences this as if somebody is taking something of him away. Then Mummy comes in with a cold drink and Mummy gives a little cuddle to Sam who's come to play. Little Sam likes this so he gets a few more hugs from Mummy. Suddenly John gets really pissed off and starts crying because in that moment he feels like he's losing his Mummy. He also identifies himself with Mummy and believes Mummy to be part of him.

This is the beginning of this whole game that, thirty years later, results in 'my story'. This story is built up very slowly, brick by brick. Later, when you are in your twenties, maybe you have a red sports car, and again it's 'my' sports car. Maybe you get a girlfriend or a boyfriend and they're 'my' girlfriend or 'my' boyfriend. So this fortress, this castle, is built up brick by brick. You don't exactly notice it because all around you other people are busy building up their fortress too. So it seems very natural. Everybody's busy with their bricks and cement.

You can see it around Arunachala. The first thing that happens is that people put a little fence around their bit of land and then they start to build up their house using bricks and cement: 'This is my house.' It probably has a front door and maybe a gate with a padlock and a bell; or maybe it has a security guard, or even barbed wire and guards with rifles. What you see on the outside is a reflection of what's actually happening on the inside.

If you go to some local village you'll find that they don't even lock their front doors, and they probably only have front doors to keep the monkeys out. And they're constantly inside each others' houses. But if you go to Los Angeles, to one of the rich areas, you find, first of all, there are tall walls. You can't even see the house. The gate has fortifications, some video cameras and a little guardhouse where they check your credentials if you want to enter.

Once we've built up our fortress then naturally we need to protect it. In our own psychology we have all kinds of defences and occasionally we let somebody come across the bridge, over the water and into our fortress. We call this person a friend and this friend is only let into the outer room, whether it's the outer room of the house or whether it's the outer room of the psychology. And then occasionally one of these friends becomes more intimate and they're allowed to come a little bit deeper into the fortress. They maybe get invited to the dining room, and in special cases they get invited to the bedroom. This is very intimate. Almost nobody gets invited there because we have to defend our fortress!

Generally speaking, the ones who get invited closer are the ones we like. What that means is that they're the ones who agree with our story. I have my story and you have your story and if your story agrees with my story then you can become a friend. If your story's very different from my story you become an enemy; no chance to come into the fortress, and I might even throw things at you from the wall of my fortress. 'Go away! Don't disturb my story.' I like my story very much. In fact, I've come to believe that this story is me. So, of course, I have to be very careful with my story and who I allow to come close to my story. 'This is a terrible person. She's always wearing pink. I can't stand pink!'

These fortresses are very well constructed and very strongly defended, and somebody like Premananda is a big threat to the fortress. He has all kinds of secret weapons, amazing electronic devices that can penetrate these defences and catch you unawares and naked in your bedroom, naked with your ideas, naked with your beliefs, in fact naked with the whole story. Premananda needs to be watched very carefully. You might even need to create some special kinds of defences because his whole effort is to get inside your fortress. In fact, he always carries in his pocket a big lump of explosive and he's always looking for a little hole where he can stick it in and blow a big hole. He's always looking for the brick that could be the one that brings down the whole castle, the foundation stone with 'I' written on it.

If we could get to this one stone – this foundation stone – the rest of the fortress could fall down very easily. Self-enquiry brings you to this foundation stone. Instead of taking the fortress down brick by brick there's a possibility of the whole thing collapsing in one moment. This fortress, which is so carefully built to keep the other people from coming in, also has the effect of keeping you from going out because you're very busy defending it. How can you possibly go out and leave the castle defenceless? Premananda might be hanging around with his explosives! Very rich people with lots of fear, living in these big mansions with high walls around, video cameras and security guards, they live not so differently from prisoners. The only difference is that they are their own jailers.

Satsang is making the suggestion that you can live your life without the fortress. You don't need it, and anyway it's only an idea. It doesn't really exist. Right now as I'm speaking you can come in touch with your own story. You may have a little pack of stories, a few different identifications, and you offer different stories to different situations. Deep down what is the fear? What are you actually defending? You're basically defending an idea that isn't true. It's a false idea. It's an idea that many people have, but that doesn't make it right.

The first step in dismantling the fortress is to be very honest and very clear. You need to be really clear about who you are and who you are not. If you see clearly that you are the Eternal Self, then you are not this story. Then you can also see there's really nothing to defend. But if you're really attached to your story and you really believe you are this story then, naturally, if somebody comes along and wants to take away one brick you will feel that you're being attacked. You will defend because this is 'me'.

Maybe you can see that if you believe 'I am a person and this is my story,' you can also believe that everybody else is a person and they also have their stories, and life becomes quite complicated. You have to decide who you're going to let in the front door and who you're going to keep out. When you look around at the other people in this retreat you can quickly decide, 'I don't like that lot, but over here, they're lovely people.' We quickly divide everybody. He's a yes and he's a no and so on and so on. To maintain this complex game requires a lot of energy and effort because you never know when somebody might come and attack your fortress. Just one word could be enough.

Are you getting some sense of the tremendous effort that's needed to maintain this story and the kind of tension you have to live in?

You must always be prepared, 'Who is going to attack me next?' and very quickly it's easy to become even paranoiac that 'they' are trying to get me. If you happen to be President Bush then you send your armies out to attack the enemy because you've heard he might have some weapons of mass destruction and he's clearly a terrible person. He doesn't notice the number of people that he put to death in Texas when he was the governor. About two or three hundred people. It was done, of course, in a very nice way; we have a legal system. We are right and he is wrong. You can see that this is the same story that goes on day-by-day in our own lives.

It's really important to see all this. This is where Awareness is very helpful. What that means is that you see a situation and instead of saying, 'That person is making me angry,' you say, 'why am I feeling angry in this situation with that person?' The reality is that nobody does anything to you. On a much deeper level we are actually creating everything that happens on the outside. We create it in each moment.

There's the story of the Buddhist monk sitting in a rowing boat in the middle of a lake. He'd gone there because he wanted to be very quiet and undisturbed. He's sitting in his boat with his eyes closed and suddenly there is a loud 'Bang!' on his boat. He opens his eyes, very angry, and he wants to shout at somebody. He discovers there's another boat, but it's empty, just drifting on the current. So that anger is totally his anger. There's nobody he can blame. And this is how we live our lives. We're always blaming the other person. Somebody is doing something to me, but it's not true.

You need to be very honest. Once you have the Awareness to understand what's happening then you need honesty to take the responsibility for what you're creating. This kind of honesty is very rare. My intention is that you see this fortress that you're living in and that you see the possibility of living without a fortress. Instead of living in Los Angeles behind a big wall with security guards you just walk across the world with a small bag, totally available and just saying hello as you go, moment-by-moment. This is real Freedom.

We're here together, we're here as very friendly mirrors. There are no authority figures here. It may look like Daddy and Mummy, but actually it's not so. Even the birds want to come to *Satsang*. We're here to help each other. We have different tasks. Setting up this room together. You might be working with people that you like or people you don't like. It doesn't really matter because both can be of benefit. In fact, the people you don't like are a little bit more useful. When things happen that you don't like you can also use that to see something about your story. When everything is sweetness and light, that's not necessarily the best mirror.

One of the reasons people become involved in spirituality is because they want to feel good, they want to be happy and peaceful. This is not a wrong idea but it has to be a real Peace, real Stillness and a real Happiness, which means no fortress. Usually there are certain bits of the fortress that are doubly reinforced, much more strongly defended. As you know, most castles have an inner tower. This inner tower is more strongly defended. Even if the enemy gets into the courtyard they can't get into the inner tower. We live our lives like this. That inner tower also has to go. We hold onto it very strongly. It is a particular belief that is so deeply held that if it is attacked, or even shown to us, it's so threatening that we defend it really strongly.

That's when a teacher is really needed to show you this particular belief. It's very common that at first a student will love the teacher: 'He's such a lovely person. I love him so much.' Then it changes because this lovely person says or does something that the student doesn't like. Then there's a little resistance. Then he says something even stronger and it touches something down in the dungeons of the tower, deep underground; then what happens is a tremendous resistance. 'He might see my darkest secret. I must defend it.' So then you find that the same student who was loving the teacher, suddenly becomes very resistant.

It's hard for the teacher because the same person that was kissing his feet one minute is attacking him the next minute. Actually it's more sad than hard because these moments of deep resistance are exactly the most valuable moments. They give you an opportunity to see what is down in the dark dungeon where you don't want to look. It's very comfortable to have a nice, sweet teacher who always makes you laugh and makes you feel good, but this can be a bit limiting. If you really want to be free you've got to be willing to see the things that you don't want to see. Actually you can't see them because these are the blind spots. To see those things you need the help of a teacher. All the teachers understand this, and when a student becomes resistant and goes away there's a feeling of a wasted opportunity; it's very often the person who is close to the teacher.

In the case of Osho Rajneesh there was a man called Shiva who was his main bodyguard. This was a special position so he got to live in a small room right above Osho's room. He was a very good-looking man. He had orange hair right down his back and he was very powerful. A very special person, always standing next to the guru. As he was a handsome man all the women of the ashram were throwing themselves at his door. He had a very nice lifestyle and everything was very good for a number of years. Then there came a time when Osho went to America and there was a different person coordinating the ashram. Suddenly he found he didn't have this special job anymore.

He became a truck driver and he became very sad. This very special person became very ordinary. Like everybody else. For him it was much worse than that. He found he didn't have his old closeness to Osho and so he got more and more unhappy, and finally he just left one night. Then he wrote a book. It wasn't a very friendly book, *The God That Failed*. In fact it was a rather unfriendly book telling all kinds of nasty things about Osho. This is a very normal pattern. In the end that man lost an opportunity to see something, something so threatening that he actually had to leave to defend it.

Probably he found another teacher, naturally a much nicer and better one, saying all the right things. For some time everything works very well until, if this is a good teacher, he'll also say something that you don't want to hear. And then the whole thing happens again. You find, in the spiritual world, a whole bunch of professional seekers. They go from one teacher to the next, but they never really look. They appear to look. They don't want to see this dark secret because there's so much fear about it. It's totally okay to become resistant, but use it as an opportunity. It's a wonderful opportunity. It's not a bad thing to become resistant, but it's really a waste when you don't use that moment.

This happened very often around Papaji. Sometimes it was very funny. I remember one day a man was sitting with Papaji. Papaji got pissed off with him. He felt he was wasting his and everybody else's time. So he told this guy, 'Go out!' And he sent him out of the *Satsang*. He did that very rarely so it was shocking. Everybody could feel that. It was almost like they were being sent out. The next day Papaji was talking to a woman and during the conversation the subject of her boyfriend came up. So Papaji said, 'Oh! Bring your boyfriend to sit with you now,' and then she said, 'Well, actually Papaji, he was the guy that you threw out yesterday.' Then Papaji laughed and there was no problem for him to come back.

There's a woman in Germany who Papaji even threw out of the town, saying, 'Go! Leave the town!' Now she gives *Satsang* in Papaji's name. It's not wrong and it's not bad if these kinds of moments happen. But be honest in that moment and have the courage to see what you were doing because the teacher is not really doing anything. Try to see it, otherwise there's a wasted opportunity and actually we don't have so much time.

This three-week retreat is really beautiful and it's really precious. We can support and help each other to see the bricks of our fortress. Use these mirrors, whether it's a little bit uncomfortable or whether it's so painful that you can't stand it; they are great opportunities. Three weeks may look like a long time, but already the first week is almost finished. It's a wonderful opportunity to use each moment to be really present.

Question:
Before, you said feelings and emotions are all the mind. I'm wondering what is the feeling of the Self? How can I recognise if it's the Self that is telling me something or if it is the mind?

You are the Self. When you're really connected to the Self you absolutely know that. The Self is something that doesn't change. The Self is the Pure Awareness.

When there's a feeling coming is this illusion?

When a feeling comes that's real, but then you attach to it and say, 'This is my anger,' then you get lost in a story. If you can say, 'Anger is happening now,' then anger is no better and no worse than some other feeling. There are many feelings, like a painter's palette, different colours. There's boredom, excitement, fear, happiness. These are all natural and there's not one that's better and not one that's worse. They're just different. As soon as you become identified with a feeling then it probably takes you into a big story. If you see it just as anger happening you'll find that it changes quite quickly. It doesn't really bite. So my advice is to completely allow whatever the feeling is.

Just imagine a life where you're always happy, it would be very one-dimensional. Rather than making constant judgements, 'This is good, this is not good, I like this, I don't like that,' you simply accept everything as it is. When you have that kind of acceptance life has an easy flow, and when you're constantly judging good and bad there's a struggle and a lot of energy goes into it. Not a great way to live.

There's a famous Spanish story about Don Quixote. He was constantly fighting windmills because he thought they were the enemy. Like this we are going through our life, but it's all happening inside of us. A little courage is needed. When things get very uncomfortable, that's when you need a little courage.

Question:
When my heart started closing more and more, one key experience for me was my meetings with Shanti. I'm very thankful for these meetings. I have a problem when people come to me with demands. I want to please them, and Shanti was attacking my fortress.

She's one of Premananda's secret agents!

Yes, she ran into my fortress.

Yes, she's also got a pocketful of explosives. She's very dangerous. She has a couple of the most dangerous things. First of all she's a woman, this is very dangerous for men, and she is also a loving woman. This makes her even more dangerous. We have to be happy that she is here.

I like her very much.

Careful! She might come and attack you. An important trick is to take advantage of all these mirrors without getting lost in them. It's easy to get caught up in somebody else's story. You have your story and the other person's story and then everything gets a little bit more complicated. I'm going to talk about love affairs separately. For me love affairs can be the ultimate illusion. It's very easy to get lost in that kind of story.

Authentic Love

Love, Sex and Relationship

Adam and Eve

Authentic Love simply is.
Authentic Love is given.
Authentic Love is your nature.
When you reside in your being,
when you reside in your True
Nature, then Authentic Love
simply is and you are that.
That's Authentic Love.
There's nothing really to do.

Authentic Love
Love, Sex and Relationship

Welcome to *Satsang*.

Authentic Love simply is. Authentic Love is given. Authentic Love is your nature. When you reside in your being, when you reside in your True Nature, then Authentic Love simply is and you are that. That's Authentic Love. Actually there's nothing really to do. Of course we have all been doing a lot and so most of us have only had small glimpses of this Authentic Love, but even those small glimpses are enough to keep the fire burning and to remind us of this possibility.

We are going to look at relationship, love and sex. Probably this is the topic that occupies the most time in our lives. Probably it is also the topic that gives us the most suffering and, occasionally, the greatest joy. We live in a world where the obsession is relationship. If you look back over your life you can see that you've always been in relationship with somebody. When we were very small we were mostly in relationship with our mother, followed by our father, our brother, sister, other members of the family. As we got older we had friends, playmates, school friends. As teenagers we might have had a boyfriend or a girlfriend. We were always relating with somebody on the outside. We didn't even really think about it because it was so natural; everybody was always busy with it.

This seemed absolutely natural; everybody was doing it. We had student friends at college or university, we got a job and there at work we had our working friends, colleagues, a boss. Of course, we still had Mummy and Daddy somewhere in the background. We still had our boyfriend or girlfriend. Perhaps that became a bit more formalised and we then had a husband or a wife.

Almost without even noticing, we are constantly in relationship with somebody. Also without really noticing it, we always assume that love will come from this somebody with whom we are relating. Mummy loved us, Daddy loved us and then our friends, then our boyfriend, our wife. There was always somebody who was supposed to love us. It was just totally natural. In fact, the whole society is set up in that way; it's absolutely formalised. Most accommodation is for families or couples and those who live alone are seen to be a little strange.

In society's view they didn't quite make it: the woman is not quite beautiful enough to have a man; the man is not quite manly enough to deserve a nice girlfriend or wife. So without even talking about it there is a sense that if you live alone you've failed, because everybody knows that the status quo is to have a partner. All of this is unspoken. There are no big signs on the street, but everybody knows the game and everybody is involved in the game; we don't even think about it.

Of course there are a few very determined people who become monks or nuns and who decide not to have a relationship. But even they are in relationship with somebody. They relate with the other monks. They are also in relationship with God, but God is separate; he is also somebody on the outside who they relate with.

Our whole focus is always on the outside. Our whole focus is always into the world looking for somebody to come along and be the person who is going to love us. Out of this tragic misunderstanding there is the suffering of always trying to find somebody who will bring us love and our life becomes a never-ending queue of relationships. We are all rather mature here and so we know that it works for some time because we have done the cycle a few times. During the honeymoon period there is a lot of hope because you have just met and there is a wonderful chemistry. Suddenly everything seems to be possible because now this one is the one, my soul mate who will be there with me, who will give me the peace, the sense of oneness that I have always longed for.

This is a wonderful dream and we keep trying to create this as reality because somehow deep inside we remember those childhood stories about the prince who came on the white horse and the princess waiting in the castle, waving. The prince is such a handsome man sitting on the beautiful horse ready to take the princess away for her whole life of happiness, love and peace. Many beautifully romantic stories are deeply embedded in our psyche. We are always out there in the world, going to the discotheque, going to the pottery class, even *Satsang* weekends, tantra workshops, wherever we go to find that perfect soul mate, the one who we can really meet perfectly.

But in all of this something is always missing. Everybody is unhappy with that kind of run-about of relationship, always trying to find the more perfect companion, but everybody is playing that game. Wherever you look there are couples talking of separation, couples who have just became separate or couples in this honeymoon phase where the hope is enormous, but the reality is really resting on thin ice.

Falling in love Hollywood style creates all kinds of dramas. Never ending dramas. Usually the reality of the relationship is that it is very dramatic because it is only a short time before we find ourselves caught up in 'my story' and 'your story' and then of course, 'our story'. So quite quickly we are caught up in three stories – my story, his or her story and the story of the relating – three stories. Before we met, when we were alone, we had just one story, my story. That was already very difficult because we believed in this story and we were absolutely identified with this story and now suddenly we've stepped into a situation where we have three stories!

When there was only myself watching my story I was busy everyday creating my movie of my life. I was also spending a lot of my day watching the old movies that I created before in my own private little movie theatre. But suddenly I have a friend; I have a close friend. She also comes in and we watch my movies together. We sit in coffee shops and we go for walks and together we go into my movies and she tells me, 'Yes that's a very sad story. Wow! That was a really exciting time.' She becomes a kind of cheerleader for my own movie, gives a lot of support for it, a lot of sympathy.

Then, of course, she turns on her movies and I watch them and give her support for her movies. Gradually, we create and build up a library of our movies – that holiday we did in Thailand together, do you remember? That was wonderful!

In the beginning it's not so complicated, but if you have been in relationship you know that after only a fairly short time it starts to get more and more complicated because suddenly you are not sure whose movie you are watching. Is it her movie or is it my movie? Is it her fault? Is it my fault? Is it our fault, and anyway what is going on? Why does he act like that? Did I do something? Is it from his old conditionings? Is it something that I am doing to him? We become completely lost in this situation, not knowing anymore if it is her story or his story or our story.

Horrible! We get more and more lost and we spend more and more time sitting in coffee shops, discussing what's happening with the relationship, going to somebody for counselling, going to tantra workshops together, even coming to *Satsang* together hoping that we can figure out what's happening. Whatever it is, we never really notice that the whole thing is happening on the outside. It's always happening on the outside, in duality. We always think we are talking to somebody. We always think we are relating with somebody and this somebody is separate from me.

To fall in love there must be somebody: somebody who falls in love with somebody else. So there is me and there is you. And as we know, when there is me and you then I am identified with my life. This creates many dramas and many stories, many beliefs, desires and longings. All of this goes together with being somebody. And this we can call falling in love – the ultimate illusion. It's the ultimate illusion because suddenly you have my story, your story and our story. Most of your life energy becomes caught up with sorting out all these stories.

The conditioning around us in the society is so strong that we even get our partner to sign a contract, 'until death do us part, my wife'. She signs. 'She is my wife. She is not anybody else's wife. She's mine! And nobody else should get any love from this woman. She is mine! She is only to love me. Sign here.' So I have a car, I have a house and I have a wife and she is mine.

When you look in the traditional cultures you can find, for centuries, that the men have a way of keeping the women. Here in India when the Muslim women go out they wear a black cloak over their dress and they cover their head. Sometimes they even wear a burka that goes right to the ground, and only their eyes are visible. Most of the time they stay at home but when they leave the house everything is covered. In Muslim countries the houses even have special windows where the women can sit looking out, but you can't look in.

In other cultures there is a similar way of keeping the woman; 'She's mine.' In Los Angeles they do it in a slightly different way. They build a big house for the woman, they give her a swimming pool and fine clothes. She lives in a golden cage, but it's not really so different because inside is the same thought pattern: 'She's mine.'

A lot of trouble in relationship begins when 'my girlfriend' or 'my wife' gives a bit of love to somebody else. Things get quite serious at that point. Let's say my beautiful wife goes somewhere and meets somebody else. This somebody else is also pretty nice, so she smiles. If I notice this I get very upset because it looks like my wife is interested in somebody else. Things start getting a little hot.

If my girlfriend or wife is a heartful, open person this might happen often because it is just in the nature of things. If your heart is open then it will happen very often and then you become one of these terrible people who are considered a little unsavoury because they always seem to have a different friend around. They're always going around loving people. Isn't that terrible!

When we add in sex, everything becomes much more powerful. If you get upset when your boyfriend or girlfriend is hugging somebody, then you get much more upset if there is sex. It's like an atomic response. The whole core explodes. In the society there's a lot of sexuality happening, but it all happens hidden underneath. In the front window it's all happy families living happily ever after, but underneath it's some other game.

Of course, if this partner, this wife, this husband, if they would go off with another person then it's a big tragedy because then I feel absolutely abandoned, alone, desperate, unhappy; my whole world has collapsed. The truth is that most of society's suffering is caused by these relationship stories, and this is not understood by most people.

I'd like to read something from my book, *Papaji Amazing Grace*. This is part of an interview with a very beautiful woman. She lived on the island of Bali and she was married to a rich Italian fashion designer. They lived in a wonderful house and they had three children. When she came to Papaji the issue for her was very much her relationship. She was always struggling with whether she should stay with her husband or leave him. Papaji would encourage her, 'Call him and tell him it's finished.' Then the next day he would say, 'Call him and say you are going to be his forever.' This went on for three or four years. In the end she decided that she would simply just surrender and just be with her husband. Then her husband came to her one day and said, 'This doesn't really work for me. Goodbye.' So she has a lot of experience with relationship and in my interview with her we particularly focused on that.

Here is an excerpt.

> For many people the question of intimate relationship with another is a difficult one. Truth seems to demand that you stand alone. Yet there is enjoyment and beauty in the company of an intimate friend. The dilemma is not really about the conflict as it presents itself objectively, but rather about what is happening inside.
>
> *Yes. Even yesterday as I was walking around Arunachala I was asking myself how to be committed in a relationship without being attached. Is it possible? Because on a human level we are somehow attached. Relationship in Truth is a very subtle*

dance. I am not sure that attachment ever goes. When you love someone there is attachment to the form. That means the body of the person.

Papaji married many people. He encouraged different people to be together, even have children. But my impression was that most of those relationships didn't last long.

It's true.

I used to wonder whether he arranged marriages just to make a paradoxical point about it all or whether he really believed in the idea of husband and wife.

He said that Westerners could learn a lot from Indians about marriage. Perhaps he was naive about Westerners and our idea about the perfect one. Indians get married and accept the way the other person is and just live with it the rest of their lives. But we are not made like that (both laugh). I'm not sure if he realised that. Maybe he thought, we put these two together and they have enough in common and enough sense so that they will work it out. He was constantly underestimating our ability to make a mess of things.

So why do we always make a mess of things? I think it starts with a wrong idea. It starts from this idea that the other one will give me love and it starts with the wrong idea that I'm not whole and complete, something is missing and I need to find the person who will fill up the bit that is missing, someone who will love me. So we are all looking around for that perfect person who will come into our lives and fill up the bit that is missing. Of course, with that wrong idea we are probably attracting somebody with the same idea. They are also looking for somebody who will fill up their hole. There is a lot of expectation in the meeting. I come to the meeting with all my stories. You come with all your stories and then after only a short time we have a relationship. We become 'us' and then we have our relationship story.

As far as I can see, relationship puts us all the time deeper and deeper into the stories we are trying to become clear of and it takes us further and further away from the Truth. In all this natural kind of relating we never notice the possibility of simply being with ourselves. Being with ourselves is very beautiful because we discover, when we spend time and become quiet enough, that inside us is what we could call Authentic Love. It's not even inside us, because actually we are this Love. It's just there. You can call it Stillness, Emptiness, the Self, you can even call it God, and we can come to it just by being quiet. In that place there is overwhelming Love flowing like a spring from the mountain.

As soon as we become quiet, as soon as we connect inside to our own nature, we discover there is a pool of Love. It's just there, it's always there. We don't have to do anything. In fact if we do anything we take ourselves further away from that Love. So why not relate with this Love? Why look for a boyfriend or a girlfriend when you could just relate with your own boyfriend or your own girlfriend who is right there. This is not really your own boyfriend or girlfriend as there is nothing to relate to. It's not a question of relationship because this Love we are talking about, this Authentic Love that we are talking about, is you. This is your True Nature.

There is no question of relationship because relationship requires some distance; it requires somebody. There is no somebody, there is just Love. You are not separate from that Love. This Authentic Love just is. It's very, very simple and because it is so, so simple we don't see it. We're so busy with this other kind of love because that is so natural. It's what we've always seen happening and so we don't notice this Authentic Love; we don't notice that by just becoming quiet we feel this Love. You can experience it just walking in the forest. You can experience it sitting by the river. You can experience it beautifully just standing outside in this wonderful nature here and you can even experience it sitting in this ashram.

We're shaken; we are kind of shaken by the beauty and power of this Love. It takes away all our thoughts and we are just Present. Nothing is happening and yet we feel absolutely nurtured. We feel absolutely wonderful; these are the moments we have been searching for our whole life. Somehow we always knew it; there inside us was this knowing because we came into the world with that. We know it. This was our first knowing as a small baby. We couldn't articulate it, we couldn't speak about it, but it was known and then somehow we lost it. We got caught up.

That's really the beauty of us meeting together in *Satsang*. When you just meet together you can't not see the truth of what I'm saying. We all know it. Sitting here together we know this and it changes our whole life because then we don't have to be always searching for a partner who is going to bring us love. We can just directly connect to that Love because that Love is always constant. Suddenly the whole mode of our life changes. We can be alone. We can be absolutely healthy and absolutely alone. We can be Free. We don't have to consult anybody. We are absolutely allowed. We can go here and we can go there. We can even have a relationship. We can even be with somebody, but the whole course of that relating changes because we are not looking to get something from the other person.

You are there with the other person just out of the joy of being together and playing together. You are not there to get something. It's just a natural coming together. It's very playful, and of course it's lovely to be with somebody, but you can be with anybody, anybody who is open. It doesn't need to be a special 'mine'. You don't need to be the owner anymore. People are not afraid if somebody is unhappy and miserable. People in society are afraid of happy people, people living in Love. It doesn't depend on any place or any relationship. It doesn't even depend on the world. Because Love is our True Nature and it's always there. It's a constant. We've learned not to trust that.

Sharing:

I'd like to invite Antar to tell his story because it's a very beautiful story. It began two days ago. The night before last he was alone in his room and he told us how there was this beautiful nothing and he had this experience of his True Nature. So now he'll take the story from this point.

The night before last was this beautiful nothing. Then yesterday, when Richard was my partner, he asked me directly if there was something between us that concerns Shanti. In that moment, I realised something about my relationship with my mother. I always had a very strong connection with her. She was my greatest love. One evening there was a party at our house, and for the first time I was aware of adults drinking alcohol. My mother was drinking and it was the first time that I didn't feel a connection with her. It was a very strong feeling. There was pain in my stomach, my heart felt like bursting and I had to cry. Later, as a teenager, I experienced the same pain when my first relationship finished.

Two days ago I felt okay when Shanti and Richard were cuddling each other. But then yesterday there was enormous pain again, this enormous story. It happened many times when relationships finished and I never wanted to feel this pain again. And yesterday, actually nothing more happened than the day before, but a big story appeared. In that moment I couldn't remember the experience I'd had the day before of the Self. It was so peaceful, it was so beautiful. I couldn't remember and all of a sudden it was totally different, only pain. The child was there; my whole story; not worthy; doing everything wrong.

I thought 'Well, I have to leave, all of a sudden, for home.' I spoke to Shanti and told her, 'This is it. I'm going home now. I'm leaving the retreat.' Well, my 'I' tried to hurt Shanti so that she would feel my pain. Just to leave her here even when we planned to spend so much time together after the retreat.

But this morning something became clear. If something is happening I should stay centred in the Self, not look outside. Then I realised that the love I felt for her, what I thought love would be, was totally different compared to this experience I'd had the day before with the Self. There was real love and I saw that a person is actually not able to love because all of this is connected to this false understanding that there is an 'I' doing something. I can see it's a total, complete illusion. When the pain comes again I just want to enquire, 'Who is it who is experiencing the pain?' I hope I can overcome this because this is the heaviest pain I've had in my life, and only because I believed this illusion.

So you can thank Richard?

Yes. Without both of you maybe I could never have seen this. Well, when I thought about last night I thought Premananda probably hypnotised Shanti!

It's all my fault!

It's your fault, yes. That idea brought me absolutely to the wrong point. Now I'm sure Premananda doesn't have anything to do with this story. Actually neither do Richard and Shanti.

It's very beautiful when you can see how this is all happening inside of you. It's got nothing to do with Shanti, nothing to do with Richard and certainly not with Premananda. It's just your story. It's all going on inside of you. It's a very beautiful two days because first it started with this glimpse of your True Nature and it took you to the peaks of the Himalayas, the snow in the sunshine. So beautiful. It has never been so beautiful. Twenty-four hours later you slid all the way down the mountain to the deep valley. Down where there's no light, just pain and misery.

Before we move on we'll give Shanti an opportunity to respond to this story. This is not her story, this is Antar's story, but somehow...

Shanti: It's also my story. Well, for me it started when Premananda said that some people believe they are not worthy to experience paradise. I'm one of them and it fits with Antar's story because inside myself the snowball got bigger and bigger, and with Richard better and better. This fear inside myself of not being worthy got larger. That was my problem that I couldn't relate to Antar. Two stories met, Shanti's and Antar's.

These stories met in the particular situation of *Satsang*. When these kinds of stories meet in a chai shop, Antar is probably in the Himalayas the next day and Shanti is in the south of India! Maybe Shanti has a new boyfriend and Antar has two or three weeks of pain.

For Premananda it's a nice story because a month ago they sent me an email to say, 'We will absolutely not come to the retreat and we will no longer be part of the Inner *Sangha* (community). The Lord has taken us in another direction and anyway, Premananda, you're a terrible person.' Now here they are and this is very beautiful you see, because not only can they understand something but everybody can understand something. This story is everybody's story, slightly different stories, but basically the same story. That's the beauty of this kind of *Satsang* community because there's enough basic love here that you feel you can share these difficult stories. Anyway, we're all going to laugh because we can always laugh at other people's stories, but if we're really honest we know this is also our story.

Interjection:
Isn't it amazing that this can happen between both of them, because they are not a couple.

This is another aspect of the story. I think this story is also telling them both something. I don't know exactly the situation, but I think they both told me some months ago that they live together but they're not in relationship. They sleep close together, but they never touch. They have a kind of *sannyasin* (renunciate) relationship. But you see, that may not be totally honest because when you have such deep feelings it may be that there is some kind of intellectual, spiritual idea there. It's not against spirituality to have sex.

I remember Papaji was once asked about sex and enlightenment and he said, 'Well, then all the eunuchs would be enlightened.' In the ancient Indian wisdom of *Vedanta* (non-dual system of Indian philosophy) you follow a certain programme as a spiritual seeker and at a certain point you become celibate. A lot of wrong ideas have come from this idea of celibacy. Thirty years ago Osho opened up the box. He quickly became the sex guru because around him there was open sexuality happening. But I'm sure his intention was that if he opened up the box everybody would quickly get tired of this game. For him, this meeting with your own True Nature is so beautiful that who cares about a girlfriend or a boyfriend? But he was wrong because everybody stayed in the game. The big attraction to go to that commune is not to go and meet God, it's a good place to meet a girlfriend or a boyfriend! We have taken his intention and we've changed it.

Sharing:
I was really astonished about Antar's reaction. Actually this is the topic for many people and especially for myself – not to run away from the pain or from what or who I think is causing the pain.

Yes, this is so important. We've been running away our whole lives. The first thing that happens when it gets painful, we leave our boyfriend or girlfriend. We know we're all in the same ocean together, and when something is not happening to me I can see that there is just a small understanding needed. It's always the same story actually, because whatever the external story, it's always because I believe I'm somebody. It's one thing to hear Premananda talking about it and a completely different thing when something happens to you.

This is the whole point of this retreat. We have enough time to come to a clear understanding. In a two-hour evening meeting there's not really enough time or support, but in a longer retreat like this we have enough time and enough support that we can help each other. It's not a great idea to just leave. For example, Petra was here only three or four days. She didn't know Premananda, she didn't know *Advaita* and she didn't really know what was going on in *Satsang*. She noticed Premananda coming ten minutes late. This was very upsetting to her and then very quickly she left. She's gone off carrying her story, her big story around authority. When you meet her at the airport to fly home you'll find that she had a wonderful time here, but she will still have that story. For those who stay there's an opportunity that when you fly back something will have changed inside. There will be a profound understanding and with that profound understanding you will be able to deal with all the stories that happen, because this understanding is fundamental to the whole thing. Everything we call life we can understand through this one understanding. That's what it means when we say Freedom. We're free of all these stories and then we also become free from the pain and suffering. So don't just leave. It's exactly the time to stay, and if this is a good retreat then everybody will come to some kind of difficult moment because, as I've said before, this is Premananda's job, to create situations that put you into your story.

So, Ram, do you have a story?

Oh yes, certainly! Who doesn't have a story?

Sita (his girlfriend) is rather popular. It's hard for us not to cuddle and kiss her and maybe then you feel something. Could that be possible?

Yes. In the beginning there was this pain, as Antar described, and now there's no pain. There's a kind of acceptance.

Interjection:
I only kiss her because she's so popular. She doesn't turn me on at all (laughter)!

Isn't it nice to have such a popular girlfriend?

Well, it's also nice if she's not popular. She doesn't have to be popular to be nice or beautiful for me.

But maybe the reasons you find her nice are the same reasons other people find her nice.

Yes, certainly. I'm interested in what you said about Osho, about love and sex. What's your opinion about this? This play to hold on to one person and the game of changing partners, does it have to do with love or is it only about having sex?

My own opinion is that the only relationship which is worth such a big energy is the relationship with God because all the other relationships give you some pleasure and some pain, and if they give you a lot of pleasure they will give you, probably, a lot of pain. Loving God is a much better deal because it's always good. So my own opinion is that it's much better to put all the energy to this relationship with God. But this is not really a relationship. It's to understand that 'I am God'. Once you really know that, then the play of life goes on and you can come to be with one woman or you may come to be with many women or no women. In a way it's not really important. The important thing is this understanding that 'I am God, I am love'.

When I was a school boy I would probably have thought, 'Oh, this is a pretty cool guy who can just walk around everywhere and love everyone and not feel anything about it.'

But it's not everyone. It's also everything because you know that you're the tree, you know you're the flower, you know that you're the river. For example, I'm very happy to see that the little black bird is still sitting on the wire after three years. I feel some beauty when I come for the silent sitting in the morning and see him there. He's always sitting on the wire. He welcomed me three years ago, and two years ago and now this year.

When you really come to know 'I am the Self, I am Love, I am God', there isn't such a big difference between the little black bird and my girlfriend. Of course there is some difference, but what happens is happening inside. When I meet this beautiful bird something happens inside and when I met that Japanese woman the other night also something happened inside. It's not so different.

128

Interjection:
So could I say it doesn't matter to you if you spend the night with a woman or with a bird? From the inner feeling?

Naturally, I have more fun with a woman than a bird (laughter)! I guess if I was a bird I'd probably prefer to spend the night with the bird!

Anyway, the point of bringing Ram here is that most of the people have the feeling that Antar's story is Ram's story. When we have these *Satsang* weekends or now this retreat, many people love Sita. You've chosen a girlfriend who many people love and so this is a strong situation for you in the same way it is for Antar. Also there's a strong possibility for you. When you talk about some kind of acceptance it has to be a real acceptance. The only real acceptance is when you know that you're not the story. Otherwise it's just a mental game. You don't really accept it. But when you really understand that you're not the story because there is nobody, and that you're whole and complete, then you're not threatened by Krishna cuddling Sita. While you are threatened by that, then you can thank Krishna because every time he hugs Sita he's giving you an opportunity to see something.

Yes, yes.

You see, you set yourself up for this lesson. When you arrived here you said, 'The reason I've come here is because I can't live without Sita for seven weeks.' You didn't say, 'I'd love to be in a *Satsang* retreat because I want to be silent for three weeks.' You said, 'I can't manage without Sita for seven weeks.' So that was the beginning of this lesson. You set yourself up for this lesson. You understand?

Yes.

The sad thing about life in the Western countries, almost every country now, is that people are so focused on sexuality and they're almost not interested in spirituality. The churches are empty and the red light districts are full. What is really going on?

I think there's more spirituality in sexuality than in churches. Through sexuality there is more between the people. Maybe there is just too little going on between the people in the churches.

On some level everybody is seeking for Truth because this is seeking for me, my True Nature. They're not seeking for that in the churches. Maybe they're seeking for it in the red light district because at least there, there is some kind of meeting.

One attraction to the red light district is that in this sexual meeting, even when you're paying for it, there's some kind of pleasure. There's some kind of small human warmth. There's some kind of release from the pain and suffering. Actually, the sad thing is that the world is really suffering because people have become so divided against themselves that most people actually suffer a lot, day-by-day. Along with sex comes money. Sex and money go together. They're to do with the first and second *chakras* (energy centres). It's really like the lowest vibration. Most of humanity is vibrating at the first and second *chakra* frequency and what is being offered here at Arunachala is the possibility of living in a much higher frequency. It's much more sensitive. It's the sixth and seventh *chakra* frequency.

For example, a rock concert is in the first and second *chakra* and if you go to a string quartet or the ballet, then you're in the sixth and seventh *chakra*. It's a completely different vibration. The world is living in materialism – money and sex. This is the first and second *chakra* frequency and the energy of *Satsang*, the energy of Freedom, of Truth is far away from that.

I remember about twelve years ago after I had this moment of realisation. At that time I was sharing a small house with a young Italian woman. She was very beautiful and it was very hot. So we didn't wear many clothes. In fact we were quite often naked. We liked each other and often we would cuddle and sleep together completely naked, but we never made love and we never had sex because at that time, for Premananda, it simply didn't work. From the moment of realisation the energy was so much up in the seventh *chakra* that it wouldn't even come down to the first *chakra*. I couldn't have sex. I became naturally celibate.

I didn't make any decision, but for about three and a half years I never had sex. I had many girlfriends and the whole community had many judgements about Premananda because I always seemed to have beautiful young women around. Naturally, they thought lots of sex was happening. But actually, the young girls liked me because I wasn't having sex. They felt safe and friendly with me.

It was just like that. Then after three and a half years I met a very hot Brazilian woman and the whole sexual thing started again. I know this is a rather uninteresting subject!

Premananda continues:

I would just like to say something about Martina. She's fourteen and naturally in the society she'd be out there looking for a boyfriend or maybe not quite yet. I find it very beautiful that she chose to come to this *Satsang* retreat. She knows she doesn't have to come to these meetings and she chooses to come here. This is her nature, she's actually attracted to this high frequency, this subtle frequency. When she goes back to Germany, then there's all the pressure of society that makes her feel she has to find a boyfriend. There was one particular weekend when she was going to come to the *Satsang* weekend and her girlfriend invited her to go to a special movie weekend. There would be a boy, she hoped, whom she'd met, but didn't have his phone number. What to do? Somehow this is always a choice. Would you like to say something?

It's like that in Germany and especially in my school class. There are three friends, girls, and they're wearing the nicest clothes. Every week they have a new boyfriend and all the boys are just chasing them, like running after them. I was always very jealous, not at the moment, but maybe when I come back to Germany I will be. I thought: 'I need this too. I need these things and I need boys.' It was always very difficult and it is still difficult. Also I notice how it changes inside me, how love and peace become more and more beautiful. I notice this every day in the silent sitting and also in Satsang. *I wanted to say thank you.*

This is a very important story. She understands the beauty of what's happening here and yet, at the same time, the society creates a strong pressure. Everybody seems to get so much fun from boyfriends and girlfriends and hardly anybody goes to *Satsang.* For somebody who is young, how can you stand against this power of society? It's not so easy.

Relationship presents us with a dilemma. We can all pretend to be spiritual. We can walk around for years with our noses in the air being very silent. But all the time there is this little bomb of relationship inside us just waiting for the moment to be ignited. The question is what to do then? Do you let it go on for the next ten years? By then there will be three children and a dog. Or do you say, 'Well, this is enough. I am not interested in this relationship story. I am actually interested in Freedom, in being free of these stories.' Either you indulge these stories or you see that your whole effort as a human being is to step out of your stories. It's not easy to step out the story of relationship because it starts with Mummy and Daddy and it's a structure that has been passed down through many, many generations. Relationship is one of the very strongest structures.

Sharing:
I see that relationships don't work. I don't know any relationship
that is really free. But I still believe in the possibility that it might
work if I keep Freedom as my priority. I don't know.

Well, everything is possible. But from what I can see the odds
against it are very high because most relationships create so much
drama. Not in the beginning, of course, because in the beginning
there is a huge hope that propels everything along. So for some
time you could say it works very well.

I've been single nearly all my life and there were times when it was
good, and times when it wasn't okay with me. Throughout these
different experiences I found my own way and there came a time
when I was really at peace with being on my own. I have been in
a relationship for the last three years. I know I can be happy and at
peace on my own, so this is no longer a priority for me. I know I am
not totally free, but I have experienced something really peaceful alone
and this gives me confidence.

I think that's quite beautiful. You're fairly young and what you
are saying is unusual for somebody your age, which is exactly the
reason I wanted you to come to this retreat. I could sense that
you came to that understanding yourself and that it gives you
strength. Maybe people can see this with Jessica. She is young, but
she manifests independence.

Did you ever feel that it wasn't okay to be alone? Did you feel any pressure from your friends or your mother or the society around you suggesting that as a young woman it wasn't really okay to be alone?

Yes. Around the time I was seventeen or eighteen I told myself, 'I should have a boyfriend. Why don't I fall in love with somebody?' Everybody else was coupling up, but then other interests developed. I wanted to learn about ecological farming. So I read a lot about this and then later my interest was travelling the world. This was more important than relationship. My dreams were about these things and not about romance. It was obvious to see that my parents' relationship didn't make them happy. They were always together and then not together, together and then not together. I could really observe what happened and also we talked it through a lot in the family. So this romantic idea never really developed. I didn't want a marriage either, not as a young child and not as a teenager. I thought it was stupid to get married because of money problems.

What Jessica is saying is lovely to hear because there must have been lots of young men wanting to be her boyfriend. Do you see how much pressure there is in the society or in the family that you should have a boyfriend or a girlfriend; that it's not really even normal to be alone? It's a very deep collective pressure in the society of almost every country, that there is something wrong with you if you are alone. You would never be the President of the United States without appearing to be a happy family man. The happiest of these family stories was John and Jackie Kennedy and their two lovely kids. You may have read those happy stories.

Camelot, they called it. Later, we were told that every lunch time John was down in the White House swimming pool with a team of beautiful young women. It was for his back problem!

Sharing from Venla and Robert after spending twenty-four hours tied at the wrists with a piece of string:

Venla: There is something embarrassing about closeness for me, no matter what kind of closeness, but I experienced much freedom and sweetness with him. It was a real tantric connection. I felt it very strongly.

Robert: Yes, we had some really nice cuddling in the night and it was very easy-going. In the beginning there was a very small notion that maybe it would be better to stay apart and just be reasonable and then ... I don't know, somehow I felt it would be nicer to be little bit tender. Yesterday during the day was also interesting for me because when we were together on the bus and when we were walking together I really felt very alone at the same time. Being tied up didn't matter. There was aloneness in a very nice way.

Venla: Yes, it was the same for me. I felt your presence, but I still felt the freedom there. So in that way it was nice to have someone close.

We still had our own space all the time so it never felt crowded. There were no stories.

I don't know if you begin to see this, but the issue is not really sex. We always say it's about sex, but I think it's not. It's about intimacy. The real fear is about coming close because as you come close there's a mirror and you feel or you see your own things very strongly in the reflection of the intimacy. If the intimacy becomes really intimate then 'you' disappear and that can also be quite scary, if not terrifying. So I think we are not really afraid of sex, we're really afraid of the melting that happens in intimacy. Maybe some of you know from your own experience that it is quite easy to have sex without being intimate; that in fact the really deep meeting is the intimate meeting. The sexual part can also be part of the intimacy, but it can also happen when things are not very intimate.

Venla and Robert spoke about a tantric meeting. When there isn't 'somebody' it's very tantric because there are two nobodies meeting. When there is no somebody there is no story. So when you have a female nobody and a male nobody meeting there is something happening, but no story. It's a different kind of happening.

Robert: I think what also made it easier in some way was that Venla is not the type of woman I would usually go for. There was not the feeling of 'I must have her', this crazy thing which then totally flips and I end up in complete shit. There is something natural in being relaxed and close and just seeing her beauty, but also with a sense of distance; a healthy distance. It gives space. It was just lovely to be close.

In the morning it was also very relaxed and flowing. Very normally we just got up and maybe there was another joke about something, like the toilet. There was not this obsessive thing of, 'Oh, now what are we going to do?'

Yes, actually very often our relationships are fuelled by our fantasy. We have a fantasy about how the man or the woman should be and we desperately go to cocktail parties until we find such a person and then we say, 'I love him' or 'I love her.'

Just by this device of randomly tying two people together there's a different meeting. Maybe this comes as a surprise, but there is a possibility of a much deeper meeting. This is because when two illusions meet it stays very much in the illusion. When we meet somebody we might not exactly choose to be attracted to then it's a different kind of meeting. If you were tied to the person you most dislike, without any doubt at all, after a short time you would find that in fact it is just nonsense, it's complete nonsense. You don't really dislike this person; they just don't fit your illusion. And similarly, by being tied to the person that you'd most like to be tied to you would see your illusion because it's quite possible you wouldn't actually like that person.

One of the problems in the normal relationship game is that people are often attracted out of their illusion. Then they get caught up together and they stay together because the other person satisfies their illusion. But the reality of the every-day meeting is that it doesn't work, and it can take years to see that because our fantasy is so strong.

It is very mature when you can meet another human being in an intimate way despite all your illusions and all your projections. This is a very nice insight from Robert.

I would like to finish with a simple suggestion for couples when they are experiencing dramatic moments.

Just sit on the couch together. Sit as close as you are comfortable and just be quiet. Make eye contact. Just by sitting together with eye contact the mind and all the dramas contained in the mind start to fade. You begin to just be there. This person who is sitting opposite has been chosen out of hundreds of thousands of people, so there is a very intimate and close bond between you just naturally. Sitting together with eye contact, things start to feel completely different. The dramas start to fade away and you are left feeling quieter and quieter until finally Love is there. It just appears. If you understand what is happening you can understand that actually it's nothing really to do with the other person. This Love is not appearing because the other one is now loving you. The Love is appearing because the drama has stopped, the thoughts have stopped, the mind has become quiet. As soon as the mind becomes quiet you start to move into the Being, into your True Nature, into Stillness, into Love, and this Love has got nothing to do with the other person. Of course, you can say the other person is a mirror, you could say the other person is a catalyst and that is certainly true, but essentially the Love that you suddenly begin to experience is your own Love. Not really your own Love because it's just Love, and the Love that you experience from inside is the same Love exactly that your partner experiences over there. This Love is just Love. I call it Authentic Love.

Devotion

Surrender, Trust and Love

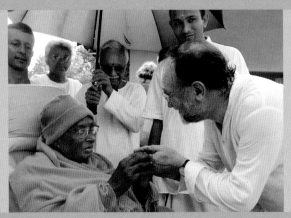

Devoted to Satchitanand

Devotion is something that
happens inside you.
The experience is happening
inside the person who makes the
offering. If you understand this and
you make an offering something
will happen. It's a subtle thing, but
it opens the heart. It encourages
a sense of surrender.

Devotion

Surrender, Trust and Love

Welcome to *Satsang*.

Everywhere you go here in India you find some kind of shrine. There you will find some pictures or statues of gods, a candle, some incense, an offering of fruit. During their day almost everybody here in India will take the time to make some devotion to their shrine. When we went into the big temple at the foot of Arunachala, we found buses full of pilgrims coming there to the inner sanctuary. This is the same in all the big temples. When people go to those holy places you notice they wear particular clothes, and in some cases the women will give their hair. This offering has a deep meaning.

Devotion is something that happens inside you. You could simply dismiss all these funny little shrines with their funny gods as mumbo jumbo, but it's not really like that. The experience is happening inside the person who makes the offering. If you understand this and you make an offering something will happen. It's a subtle thing, but it opens the heart. It encourages a sense of surrender.

You've been to the *samadhi shrine* (grave of a saint) in Ramana Ashram. You've seen the beautiful flowers there. In the early morning, around five o'clock, they make the decoration fresh each day. There are special people in the temples to do that. Devotion is a particular quality of love. It's a cool love maybe, or a compassionate or impersonal love. It's love without a story, and it's totally profound; we're not very good at it in the West.

During the bus tour we will meet five Indian gurus. The devotion to them is not so visible or extroverted, but you will feel that the people around these gurus are completely devoted to them. If they weren't devoted they wouldn't be there. The ones that the guru invites to come closer are the ones who have this devotional openness; he invites them, not because he needs to be loved in this way, but because he knows that this open heart creates a possibility.

Fundamental to devotion is an acceptance of what is. Something happens and you accept it, even if you don't like it for whatever reason, whatever judgement, or idea. This already sounds very uncomfortable and challenging, but it has an enormous effect because if you continually surrender your personal wanting then you find that all your judgements and ideas, desires and comparisons start to go away and you feel closer to the Self, closer to God, closer to your own Essence. It just happens. While you're busy in your personal 'I', being right, you're keeping yourself away; you're creating separation.

This love between the disciple and the guru, or the devotee and the Master, is very beautiful. The love that manifested in the years I spent with Osho, and then later Papaji, was the most profound of my entire life. What I'm talking about may not be very comfortable for most Western people, but for some it will be completely right. Usually this feels more natural for women. The experience of having a child also has a lot to do with surrender. Men don't know this and for them it's not so easy to surrender to somebody, particularly not to another man.

Tonight there will be this very special manifestation of devotion. Already now people have begun walking around Arunachala and as the day goes on more and more people will come. In the evening this road will be solid with people, and this flow of people will continue all through the night. Thousands upon thousands of people will be walking barefoot; women in their best *saris*, many of the men wearing only a loincloth and a *lunghi* (length of cotton cloth), walking in silence with their focus on the mountain. It's an intensive energy. I recommend you to also walk around Arunachala in this flow of humanity.

Throughout India there are many such strange devotional expressions. There is a town called Vrindavan, south of Delhi. This was the home of Krishna. You have heard of the Hare Krishna temple in Vrindavan. There are certain holy places there where Krishna was supposed to have been. The people will come there and prostrate full length, then stand up and then prostrate again. In this way they travel one or two kilometres, each time putting their forehead on the ground. When you watch this you can feel something. There is another famous place, Varanasi on the Ganges. This place has a special meaning for Hindus and thousands of pilgrims come there and take a bath in the Ganges. In the early morning, at sunrise, the side of the river is full of people bathing.

Just keep in mind when we go on the tour that all these things can look a little strange on the outside, but the effect is inside. Give it a try! Give somebody a garland. Prostrate on the ground before a shrine or one of the Saints. Say *namaste* to someone. Maybe you don't know it, but this greeting, *namaste*, which means hello, really means 'my higher Self meets your higher Self'. This is very beautiful.

Last year on our bustrip when we met Dayananda he was planning to leave his ashram at five o'clock the next morning. I told everybody in our group that he was leaving and that maybe they would like to come and say goodbye. A few people woke up early and came there to see him. However, everybody except for myself missed it. You have to tune in. Nobody is going to make an announcement. You can be sure when Dayananda leaves, all his closest people are standing there saying, 'Goodbye, *namaste*.' Those two or three minutes have a devotional meaning. This is something that we as Westerners can learn about. The effect of this devotion is that something becomes open. In this opening, something happens to our Fortress. When you are devotional it's hard to maintain the Fortress.

We can compare Self-enquiry with devotion. When you have some thought, you ask yourself, 'Who has this thought?' 'Me.' 'Who is me?' And this enquiry takes you from that thought – some object, some person, back to the Source. The way of surrender or devotion is that you simply give yourself to that moment, in the acceptance of what is. That takes you directly to the Source, the same Source as you are taken to through Self-enquiry.

During Ramana Maharshi's lifetime you can find that the people who were close around him were practising Self-enquiry, but they were also completely devoted to him. I would suggest the strongest possible path is a deep commitment to the way of *bhakti* (devotion) and the way of *jnana* (knowledge). Both together bring you into Truth and the one that suits you the best will be the one that you find yourself feeling most connected to. The way of enquiry is a little cool. The way of the heart is more hot.

Naturally when you start to surrender it involves trust. Surrender and trust are absolutely connected. We are not so good at Trust. We are good at trusting our own Fortress, but this is not exactly the trust I'm talking about. Trust means to trust what is, even when it doesn't seem to fit with our idea, and of course this is a little tricky for Western people.

If you lived with Chairman Mao Zedong, or in Russia with Stalin, naturally those experiences would make it difficult to surrender. In our daily life we have many experiences that teach us not to surrender and not to trust. You have probably discovered in your own relationships with men or women that not much can happen with a new person until you come back into trust in your heart. Many of us have experienced emotional shock in relationship and we hold this shock inside our heart for many years. Because of that shock and because of that holding we're simply not available to be loved or to love.

My friend who was here for lunch yesterday made an interesting comment. He said, 'You know, Premananda, all this work you are doing with people, it just heals them to the point where they are ready to start the real spiritual work.' Of course, there is some truth in that. We've been together for nearly two weeks, a wonderful group of people. Maybe you would not admit all the people into your Fortress; anyway, not to the inner part of your Fortress. But why not just decide that you're going to trust everybody? Why not decide that on this next part of the retreat you're going to do a small experiment and be absolutely open? It was really terrible that your father did those nasty things to you and it's very unfortunate that Mummy didn't love you more, but so what? Right now be open! She's not here right now. Your father is also not here. Why carry them along? How long are you planning to carry them? Your whole life? Naturally, after what Daddy did how could you ever trust a man again? But is that a good position? So the invitation is to simply be here and accept what is.

Question:
Tell me something about the devotion towards a guru or a Master. When you are in the Presence of a living Master it's not difficult at all to be devoted, to trust, to surrender, to worship.

He probably doesn't want you to worship him.

I didn't mean worship. It's more about devotion and being open.

Yes, he would like you to be open. He would like you to be devoted, but not to him personally. He is not asking you to be devoted to his habit of putting his finger in his nose. He would like you to be devoted to the Self, your Self. When you bow down to the guru you are not bowing down to him as an individual person, but you are being devoted to the Self of the Master. The Self of the Master is your own Self. There is only one Self.

Yes. What happens after the Master has left his body? Is there a transmission from the Master to the devotee?

No, the Master is not being devoted to you; you are being devoted to him. Whether he is living or not, you can be devoted. Many people who never met Ramana Maharshi are devoted to him. This devotion is about what happens inside you. I was very devoted to Osho and then at a later time, after he had died, I came to Papaji and became directly devoted to him. I made a ritual to say goodbye to Osho and consciously said, 'Goodbye and thank you.'

The fifteen years I spent with Osho were very important for me, so I wanted to thank him for that. I wanted to become clear that I was saying goodbye because now my devotion was directed to Papaji. It doesn't mean that I don't love Osho. I'm very grateful to him. I have a stronger devotion to Papaji, but actually my deepest devotion is to Ramana Maharshi, who I never met. Hence, this retreat is happening here.

That's also what's happening in myself.

You have been devoted to Osho for many years. I suggest that at some point it's very healthy, and probably necessary to say, 'Thank you very much. Goodbye.' Many *Osho sannyasins* (disciples of Osho) find this very difficult and then they can get stuck. This same man who came for lunch yesterday was commenting on the people who are here from Lucknow who were very close to Papaji.

They haven't changed for ten years; they are even wearing the same clothes. There is some truth in that, because it's easy to get a bit stuck. It's important to remember that we're interested in Truth and the guru is pointing to the Truth. Don't get caught on his finger. Remember what he is pointing to. Occasionally, I suggest that *Osho sannyasins* might burn their pictures of Osho. This advice is always very unpopular!

Yes, I feel it's okay. I only have my mala *(prayer beads) in my house, and I never feel unhappy because Osho is no longer here. It touches me when you say that 'thank you and goodbye' can be devotional. I start seeing now what devotion really is. Thank you.*

Question:
How do you know that you have found the right guru, the right teacher?

I would say that you simply know. How do you know when you find the right girlfriend? It's really clear, even though she may not be the one you thought you would be ready to be with. When I went from Osho to Papaji, I went from a guru who arrived in a stretch Rolls Royce, onto a white marble platform, wearing beautiful clothes and was surrounded by beautiful women, to a man who came in a van, with tattoos on his arms, wearing an old T-shirt. He seemed a lot less then my first guru. But I already knew that this meeting was going to be very important and something just happened inside. Maybe it is important that in order to meet the new guru you must say goodbye to the old guru.

When I met you in Copenhagen you weren't quite sure if you wanted to come to the weekend with Premananda because you had recently left another guru, or he'd left you. At that moment you'd had enough of gurus. But you did come to the weekend and now you are here. Against your own idea you are here, and the other morning you wanted to have a new name. I said, 'Well, I can give you a new name, but it has the meaning that you take me as your teacher,' and then you didn't want to have a new name. Surrender is an issue for you. When you ask for a new name I'll know that you have resolved the issue.

Okay. I can say there has been quite a lot of resistance during the retreat and, of course, I have considered that it's my inner struggle, Mein Kampf, *my fight.*

In the movement of time you just naturally know to say 'goodbye' and to say 'hello'. I consciously made a little ritual of saying goodbye to Osho because I felt that would allow me to be more intensely with Papaji. Papaji never asked that and he would never ask that. As I said before, the people who are the most surrendered are the ones you find closer to the guru. The guru is not choosing the people who are closest. They choose themselves.

But it doesn't feel right to surrender to you.

Nobody's asking you to surrender to me. What is being suggested is you surrender to what is. You have chosen to come to this retreat and there is a certain flow, which means that tomorrow morning we are going on a bus tour. You have some concerns about the lack of silence but you may be surprised to find that you can even be silent on a bus. The real issue seems to be about Premananda.

Yes, I agree.

So in that case my advice would be you absolutely should stay for the bus tour and in the retreat.

I don't agree.

Well, then you will make your own decision. (Later he left the retreat for another teacher.)

Question:
You said before that surrender and trust are always connected.
So if a person seems unable to surrender to something or someone
could it be that he cannot trust himself?

Yes, it's always about yourself, not somebody else. Our Danish man's issue is his issue. It's not really about Premananda, even though he would like to make it about Premananda. I can feel his resistance, and anything I say to him is likely to increase his resistance. He has a strong authority issue and now it plays out.

Is it right that surrender is only possible while we are staying in
Presence?

The true surrender is when you are present. When you are present, not caught in the conditioned mind, then there is the Self. That's surrender. You can't do surrender. You can't have the idea, 'I'm going to surrender to somebody.' It just happens.

Question:
Sometimes the inner resistance is very strong. Right before Satsang
I had this strong feeling to just go away.

I think everybody here has had that feeling. We've spent our whole life going away. It's a very common pattern.

Yes. I am grateful that I am still here, and I realise that it frightens me that we all go together on the bus tour. Also I'm very happy about it.

In the last days we have been looking at the Fortress, the ego. We've been focusing on things that people usually prefer not to look at. One woman came to see that if she wants to live in Truth then something will have to change in her relationship with her boyfriend. She had the idea, 'Well, I'll have to leave him,' which may or may not be true. Then she experienced very strong stomach cramps. That might be because of the water or the food. Later she saw it was because she is holding on to this boyfriend in her stomach. In this kind of situation the easiest thing is to go away, and the hardest thing is to stay and deal with whatever the issue is that is cramping her stomach.

I also have this feeling in my body. There is something that is afraid.

Two months ago in our community we had a four-day retreat. People sat blindfolded and we brought them food, took them to the toilet, gave them some exercise; everything was done blindfolded. In that sitting one lady met something that was very strong for her. She was vomiting into a bucket. She was sitting blindfolded. Nobody was doing anything to her. She had to accept that it was all to do with her.

These structures of the conditioned mind are exactly the things that prevent us from simply being. We all have different structures. For most of us there is an enormous fear of just being because when we just be, this Fortress dissolves. It feels a lot like death, and then there's a possibility of enormous Love in which the Fortress can't exist. Nothing exists. In this retreat there is the possibility to find out for yourself that you are nothing. That's not very comfortable. Some people become absolutely terrified about it.

I feel it drives me a little bit crazy.

Yes, be crazy.

Sharing:
For me it's quite a different story. The last few days I've really enjoyed the dissolving structures, although my haircut was quite challenging and still is. I feel myself more and more in Peace and in Stillness. I really appreciate the stories from yesterday very much and afterwards I wrote my own story about my sexuality. I don't have to tell it now and I feel more and more quiet, although sometimes I also don't appreciate everything. But when you were talking this morning about surrender I realised I have surrendered very much.

I would say that is very clear.

For me it's strange because I gave it a lower priority at the beginning of the retreat. I really think it is true that now I feel a lot of surrender. I can see it's growing (chuckles).

Question:
You explained before that you know when you find the right guru.
You just know it in the same way you know when you've found the
right partner. This makes it really difficult for me. There were some
situations in my life where I thought I'd found the right partner,
but I was totally wrong.

Yes, but it's always the right partner. Is there really a perfect partner? There's the partner that's happening right now and that partner right now is the perfect partner, right now.

If I consider my time with Osho I could find a lot of reasons why he wasn't the right guru. But actually, he was absolutely the perfect guru for me at that time. I was very impressed by his Rolls Royce, beautiful women and white marble stage. I needed a special guru at that time. I probably couldn't have surrendered to Papaji. I doubt it would have worked. I needed the fifteen years with Osho in order to be ready to meet Papaji. So although I could easily have some criticisms about Osho, now, looking back on him, he was really perfect for me at that time. He completely changed my life by showing me, by his Presence, that something different was possible.

This question, 'Which is the right guru?', really keeps me busy, even
before I met you.

Let's say the right one is the one that challenges you.

So the guru you are with right now is always the right guru?

We met in Gottingen six months ago. It was a particular moment for you. You were very open and our first meeting touched us both. You even surrendered your moustache at one point. But since then the surrender has gone.

When I came here there was a strong connection to Premananda and right in the beginning I had an opening of the heart. One morning you were sitting there on the couch and I was looking at you. You had your eyes closed, and then I could feel this very strong love for you. It was very beautiful for me to discover it. It was the first time I experienced this strong feeling of love for you and it's not very easy for a man to tell this to another man.

In the last days my experience here in the retreat changed and the question came, 'Ah, these are really nice little games we are doing here, but is it really necessary? Shouldn't we just be quiet?'

These nice little games don't stop you being quiet.

That's right. More and more stories are coming up. This doesn't fit my feelings right now. I would wish for more silence.

I would wish more silence for you. I sensed there had been a few moments in the last days where things got a bit uncomfortable for you. It's a nice idea that it should be more silent.

157

No, I can't say this, Premananda. The positive effect I noticed was that stories started to get boring for me.

That's already very positive. You're talking about being quiet more often. There's plenty of time to be quiet. I would be very happy if the retreat became quiet. I would be very happy if there were no more stories. It has to be real silence from within and that is only possible when the stories stop.

I know a man who spends six months of every year living in Italy and six months living here. He is very spiritual. I don't doubt that he often goes to Ramana's cave, but nothing really changes. He still lives with the same girlfriend and fights with her everyday.

On the one hand I am very quiet, more quiet than at home and I enjoy it very much, and on the other hand there is a critical way of looking at what is going on here. So the question comes back, would it be different in another retreat with another teacher?

I hope it would be different. My advice would be to absolutely surrender to what is happening and then see how that affects you inside and try to be honest to see those things.

Yesterday I was alone in the town and it was a very strong experience for me. Suddenly I was standing there in the midst of all that chaos and it became very quiet inside and I felt like everything was melting together. It was only a few minutes, but it felt absolutely great for me. Then my mind started again, wanting to grab it or wanting to analyse it and understand what happened. Then it was gone.

I want to tell you something from my own experience about self-awareness. Earlier you said you were bored and things got on your nerves, but you didn't see that as resistance or something challenging to look at. I know this for myself. I often have the feeling, 'Oh, this is really boring now, the same stories and the same questions again.' Often my response towards something is boredom. But I found out for myself that this boredom is just an excuse to run away. Because when I say, 'Oh, this story is really boring,' then I don't take responsibility for my response.

That means that I am not present and that means that I project. Then I simply project something onto the other person and I think it hasn't anything to do with myself. But this is absolutely not true because everything has to do with myself. Everything is my mirror. If someone is telling a story that I find really boring, then it's really uncomfortable to say in this moment, 'So this has something to do with me.' This is my experience and maybe you can see that the challenge is exactly that which gets on your nerves. Because the things that get on your nerves, they move something inside of you. Then for sure, you could say, 'Why does it affect me, why does it touch me?

I don't experience it like this at the moment, because I can feel the difference between boring and challenging. So let's take the example of my moustache. Shaving it off was really a challenge and this boredom feels totally different. It has to do with the stories we were listening to yesterday. I hear stories like these very often in my psychology practice. I am very used to looking at what these stories touch inside. For sure there could come the impression that it's boring because I don't want

159

to look at it, but I think it is more the wish to be in silence and not to listen to stories I've heard many times. Even though I value the people who were talking, at the moment there is no longing for stories.

If you want to be quiet, then be quiet.

Yes. I want to do it, but then all this talking really disturbs me so I would have to go into the cave.

But then be honest about why all these stories disturb you. Why don't you simply sit in silence and let someone else talk? That has nothing to do with you.

Maybe it has to do with an idea that this retreat should be more in silence. Maybe it has to do with some people I met who are taking part in another retreat. There it's obviously much more quiet, and every day little miracles happen.

Nothing's happening here, of course. Not to you anyway. I feel you are incredibly protected right now and actually, not really reachable. I would guess it would be very, very threatening for you to have your hair cut.

But it can't be threatening for me because it is not an issue for me. You can Wake Up with or without hair.

Well, can I offer you the possibility to Wake Up without your hair then?

Thank you very much, but I choose to keep it.

I want to say if it really doesn't matter for you to cut your hair, then I really ask myself why you protect yourself so much against it. I can understand that with or without hair you can Wake Up. Silence doesn't depend on anybody. Even if it's loud around you, you can be in silence.

I want to invite Tanzen, our motorbiker who looks more like a Russian sailor with that hat on, to come and speak. Okay, so what would you say to this gentleman in the white clothes with the beautiful hair?

Tanzen: The first thing is, if you would cut off your hair I would give you this little hat as a present (laughter).

Oh, honestly I don't like it so much.

Tanzen: I can remember the Satsang *about getting rid of your moustache and there I already noticed a resistance from you. This was a very small resistance compared to the one today.*

Just wait. Just try to absorb what is being told to you because you're actually somebody who we love very much and, in my opinion, this is quite an important moment for you. So just try to hear what he says without responding.

Tanzen: It looks like you can't let go of something and actually the hair and the moustache are only two little things. You told us how much nice furniture you have at home, also a very beautiful car and a very beautiful girlfriend and in order to Wake Up you have to let go of all of this, not only the hair.

I heard something else about it. There are very serious teachers who say you can even Wake Up with a lot of furniture, with a house and with a car.

You can if you are not attached to it. My sense is that these different items that Tanzen is talking about are all important bricks in the creation of your Fortress. If we were right about you being a three in the *Enneagram* (a diagram of character fixation), then this is a lot about image and this natty little non-sports car that looks like a sports car would be an extension of your Fortress. Possibly also the girlfriend. Possibly the house and possibly the hairstyle.

If you are not attached to those things then, naturally, they don't in any way come between you and your Awakening. But if they are part of your image of yourself, part of your film, then they will get in the way of your Awakening. Only you know that. But I remember in our very first meeting you told me about the furniture, and it seems as if these objects that you have surrounded yourself with are in fact part of this created Fortress.

The thing that you are really resistant to letting go of in this moment is your sense of yourself. So I would guess there's a very good chance that all these things that Tanzen referred to are props in the movie. About three years ago, in a cave up on the hill, I met a woman who was sitting there in *samadhi* (state of absorption),

162

very blissful. She had a younger man taking care of her. He would walk down and get water and food and take it back to the cave.

I was very touched from meeting her, so for some months I paid somebody to take water to her. Now she is living just over there in a very nice house and I don't expect that it has any affect on her *samadhi*. Is that really true for you?

No, I found out already that it's not true for me and, as I told already, slowly I start to empty the cellar…

Very slowly.

I realise that it's very difficult to let go of things and I realise that I built up this cage very nicely. It's really difficult to give up this comfortable cage. But then there are these moments when I find out that this lifestyle bores me and hurts me.

Yes, you have to be a bit honest here. About six months ago you came to *Satsang* in Munich and you were talking about coming to live in our community and giving up your house. This was the same moment when Arjuna came to *Satsang*. Now, six months later, Arjuna is living in our community. He gave up his house, he gave up his job in Cologne and at the time he even gave up his wife and moved to the community. In that six months you have taken out a few old pieces of furniture and you have lost your moustache. So you are slowly moving in that direction. But I doubt that you will get to our community because anybody can see that it's not comfortable.

And maybe you also remember that from the beginning I said that giving up the house and the practice is not something that will happen in six months. It is something that will take some time. Arjuna gave up an apartment and for me it's a house with three levels.

Three levels! Maybe we'll come and live in your house! You can just stay there. We would like the furniture too. We'll make friends with your neighbour.

Yes, for sure (laughter).

Then you don't have to give up anything.

I now have the opportunity to meet the community and get to know everyone, and it's true, I don't find it so comfortable.

If you were really honest you'd have to see that things like comfort are very important to you. You have many ideas that are very important. You have a house and other things that are also very important and together there is a real sense that surrender is quite a strong issue for you. Most of the people here would feel there is a strong resistance happening. You will find that life will get much more interesting for you in this boring old retreat when you start finding out what this resistance is about. We're about to go on a bus trip for four days. You don't have to speak even one word.

What is important for Awakening? Holding on to our false self-image probably won't bring Awakening. Although you found the last few days a bit boring I would say that for most people it has been quite a challenging time, that maybe for the first time they have seen more clearly what it means to live in stories. As a psychologist you are listening everyday to many stories. This doesn't always give you the best experience to see your own stories, as I think everybody would feel right now. I invited Tanzen to speak to you because I have a headache.

My headache is related to your resistance and I wanted you to hear this from other people because this is exactly the kind of situation when our clever, defending, conditioned mind makes the teacher wrong. You may be doing that right now. This is where the reserves from our heartful meetings are very important, and we have those. The other morning you felt much love, and exactly in these kinds of moments the heart connection becomes very important. In the last forty minutes we have been bashing on you very strongly and it's not so comfortable. Hopefully it will change the retreat from boring into something more exciting!

Sharing:
Premananda, I am very glad about your talk this morning because so far what you have been talking about is rather familiar to me. I was also thinking not to go on the bus trip. When you were talking about the adoration for the things in the temples I was thinking, 'Oh no, that's not for me.'

Then you talked about surrender and you touched something very deep in me. All of a sudden, I saw that this is the point I have been looking for. We all want to Wake Up but I didn't know how and I didn't know what was keeping me away from this. If I look back, I see that I have always been running away from surrendering to myself. So this was a good discovery and all of a sudden everything changed and I said fully 'yes' to going on the trip.

Just see that this trip is not about four days sitting in a bus. This trip we are talking about is your whole life. People go through their whole life resistant. They don't like it because it's raining. They don't like it because it's too hot and they don't like what is. You understand?

Yes.

This is keeping them always separate and always in resistance. So it's very beautiful what you say.

Thank you.

Destiny

Divine Plan, Just Life Itself!

Courtyard Satsang at Open Sky House

When we simply surrender it's a
bit like a piece of wood floating in
the river. Everything gets very easy
and without really doing anything
things seem to work out — maybe
not in the way we thought, but in
another way. If we can accept that
as it is, then life is very easy.

Destiny
Divine Plan, Just Life Itself!

*Destiny brought me to Leipzig and this talk was given exactly
two years later on my return to Germany from the Arunachala
Retreat.*

Welcome to *Satsang*.

Tonight is a rather nostalgic night because it's exactly two years
since I first came to Germany, and through some strange destiny
I arrived in Wolfenbuttel which is in a forest a bit north of here.
Ten days later I was here in Leipzig having a meeting like this
and for the first year Leipzig became the focus of my travelling
in Germany. So tonight I am planning to tell you some of the
stories about Premananda in Germany because it makes a very
interesting point about destiny.

Most of us have the belief that I'm doing my life. Day-by-day we
have the idea that we are doing what happens and we are making
it happen in freedom. Leipzig is in the old East Germany so most
of you probably remember the exciting revolution in 1989 when
this wall between East and West Germany came down. I wasn't
here, but I guess there was a feeling of freedom.

It's interesting to look now at what has happened to this freedom.
You are free to travel anywhere in the world. But is this really

freedom and is there any difference between what happens now and what happened twenty years ago? There are some obvious changes, but twenty years ago everyone thought that 'I'm doing my life' and now we still wake up each morning with this same idea. We probably also wake up with the idea that there is somebody to do this life. We call this 'me'.

This meeting is to look at this idea of me doing my life. We always assume it's true: me and my story, my life, the ongoing day-by-day drama called my life, and we naturally assume that I'm doing this. Anyway, I'm free. But are we really free? This meeting is about a quality of freedom that is not dependent upon any political boundaries. Surprisingly, we might find out that it's possible to be absolutely free even when our body is locked up in prison. In the same way we might find out we can be absolutely not free even when our body is free to go anywhere.

When I left India and my spiritual Master twelve years ago, I went straight to jail in Thailand. I left India and was arrested the next morning in Bangkok airport. I spent the next three weeks in three different jails. It even included being shackled in leg irons and wearing a little brown monkey suit, holding my chain and sitting in a cage waiting to go and sit in front of the judge. Yet, I was still free. Nothing really changed. Of course, Premananda would have much rather been on the beach in Goa than holding the chain in a Bangkok prison. However, what's really essential never changes.

Ramana Maharshi said that if you have an idea to do something and you aren't meant to do it, it won't happen. And equally if you have an idea about something you don't want to do, but you are meant to do it, it will happen. This is directly opposite to our idea about 'me doing my life' because it is suggesting that there is a Destiny at work and that we are merely grains of sand blowing in the wind. This is not very comfortable if you are very attached to this guy who is doing my life.

If you have never been to one of these meetings before your mind may be slightly concerned, wondering if you have come to the right place tonight. Equally, if you have been to this kind of meeting before and you have slightly forgotten what it is all about you might feel excited, because if this idea of Destiny is correct, there's a possibility of simply surrendering to that, which actually means you don't have to do anything. You simply accept what is, even if it is exactly what you don't want to do, even if that's the last thing you want to do.

This is why Premananda's own story is interesting. For thirty years I had a very strong opinion that I didn't want to come to Germany, not even to visit. Amazingly, even though I definitely had no plan to come, a French woman brought me to Wolfenbuttel two years ago and now I am living in Germany. I even have a German car, and in fact I actually have a nice time here. My mind can't really understand this. I have a great time everyday. So how is this possible?

It can only be possible when you simply let go, when you give up your own idea. Four years ago I was living in Sydney, Australia. It was the end of December and I was packing up my car to go and give a *Satsang* retreat and have a bit of a holiday on the beach. You probably know Australia is a bit strange. It's exactly opposite to Germany. In Australia January is like August. Everybody goes on holiday and they have Christmas on the beach. So I was heading off to the beach and suddenly, very unexpectedly, there was this very clear message that I would be leaving Sydney, leaving Australia and that's it. I was quite open to this idea because I had lived in Australia for six years and it felt like enough. I had some interest to go to Europe but I hadn't been there for sixteen years, so it was a very unknown place. I didn't really know anybody, so I didn't have any idea how it was going to happen.

I went from Australia to India. Just before I was leaving the small Indian town where I had been living for a year and a half to fly to Europe, I met a man in the street. He told me that a year before, in India, he had been to my meeting. I had said something that was really helpful for him and he wanted to thank me for that. I told him that I was coming to Europe and that a French friend was bringing me to Wolfenbuttel. He said, 'Oh, why don't you come to Leipzig? It's not far from Wolfenbuttel. But I don't know if anybody in Leipzig would be interested in *Satsang*.' Anyway, I came here exactly two years ago and as far as I know it was the first *Satsang* in Leipzig. Maybe some of you were there at that meeting. Susan is here and she was the hostess for that first meeting because her boyfriend at that time was the man I met in the street in India.

Here I am, two years later, back in Leipzig and the idea I had about Germany has completely changed. After two years I know many,

many people and almost every weekend I spend with about thirty people. I'm living on a beautiful farm in the south of the Black Forest with sixteen friends, three kids, three or four cats, a donkey and fifty horses. I travel constantly around Europe. Nothing like that was planned at all.

Actually, the other nice bit of this story is that Premananda's mind thought it would be nice to go to England. I'm English and my parents are quite old, about eighty-five now. I have spent the last twenty years travelling around, but not in England. So Premananda's mind had this nice romantic idea about spending a few years with his old parents, you know, before they departed. So I wrote them a letter saying: 'I'd like to live down the road so I can easily come and visit you. Wouldn't that be nice, we haven't seen each other for so long.' Then I called them from India to say, 'Well, you know Dad, I'm coming to Europe and I think I'll come and see you and maybe I'll live down the road,' and he said, 'We don't want to meet you.' (Laughs) So you see, this is a really good example of what Ramana Maharshi was saying.

Then I have a choice, 'I don't want to live in Germany. I would like to live near my parents.' Do I try to make that happen or do I simply surrender? When we try to make things happen life usually gets very dramatic and it's a constant battle, a constant hassle. When we simply surrender, it's a bit like a piece of wood floating in the river. Everything gets very easy and without really doing anything things seem to work out – maybe not in the way we thought, but in another way. If we can accept things as they are then life is rather easy. The difficulty is that we have such a strong identification with 'me', 'my life', 'I'm doing it'. If you have any interest to live in Peace, Harmony and Love the simplest way is to completely surrender to what is. Of course, this is not so easy because we have a lot of attachments to our own ideas; to 'me'.

When we stay attached, life gets very dramatic. If we can simply let go then we can move in the flow of the river of life and trust where we are going. It doesn't matter where we are going. It's really about the journey, not about the destination. If I enjoy the journey from moment-to-moment in Harmony and Peace then actually it doesn't really matter where I'm going because when I get there it will still be Harmony and Peace. This is very challenging if we have the idea 'I'm doing my life' because naturally we are very attached to that. We probably have an idea of the destination and we are very busy moving our life to that destination.

In our everyday life we're constantly being offered opportunities to see our attachments. I want to go for a picnic tomorrow at lunchtime. There's a wonderful park in Leipzig, but maybe it's going to rain. So what about this idea? 'Oh we'll take umbrellas, but I'm going to have my picnic!' We can end up on the grass with our umbrellas with water and mud everywhere or we can simply have a new idea. It doesn't really matter. Freedom is not about doing what I want to do. Freedom is really about being in Harmony and Peace, and that doesn't depend on anything because that is your nature. You don't have to do anything for that. In fact, it's only really available when you don't do anything. If you're trying to do something then you are in the drama of 'my life' and you believe in this 'somebody' who is trying to become peaceful. You don't realise that you're already Peace; that Peace is your nature.

If you really look at your life you will probably find that all the important things have actually just happened, they didn't come out of some great Master Plan.

A Sharing Dialogue:
I have tried living like that, I tried to let myself go.

Yes, but hang on, 'I tried to let myself go.' Doesn't that sound like hard work?

But I did it. I let go all my obligations, I didn't do the things I should have done. Then I came to realise that I was going round in circles. There was no development anymore.

Yes, because there was one thing you didn't understand and you were still carrying the 'somebody'. You still had the idea that there's somebody: I, me, my story. What surrender means is that you realise it doesn't work like you thought it worked. Then it's not that 'I' am going to surrender, but you suddenly realise that there's nobody to surrender and that there never was and this big

175

drama we call 'my life' was a complete illusion, no different really from what we see in the movie house. It's been playing in 'my mind' and I have been the only spectator. When you really see this there is a completely different quality to life.

When Premananda came here to Leipzig two years ago somebody said, 'Oh, why don't you come to Dresden? I'll organise a meeting in Dresden.' Then during that meeting somebody said, 'Why don't you come to our community?' I didn't have anything else to do, so I said, 'Okay, why not?' Because for me it doesn't really matter where I go. If right now you said, 'Why don't you come to Warsaw?' I would say, 'Okay. I have a spare week in June, how about that?' I don't change whether I am in Warsaw or Leipzig. It's exactly the same. I don't depend on Warsaw or Leipzig.

This is very challenging. We can say, 'Well, you know, I'll just put my foot in the water, then, you know, that's kind of okay because if it's too hot or too cold I can take it out again.' But that's not surrender.

There's a wonderful story about the life of a Sufi Master. This is not a true story, it's a sort of romantic version. Anyway, a man was working in a government office and one day he got this inner message: 'Leave your job and meet me down by the river.' So he resigned and all his friends said, 'What are you doing? This is a secure job for the rest of your life and you're just giving it up for no reason.' Then he went to that place by the river on the appointed day and at the appointed time. The inner message came again: 'Jump into the river.'

So he jumped in the river and then he realised he couldn't swim, but in that moment a fisherman pulled this guy into his fishing boat saying, 'You stupid man! Why did you jump in the river when you can't swim?' And then he said 'Would you like a job?' So for some years he became the assistant to the fisherman and then again this inner voice came and told him to leave everything and go some other place. He kept doing this and finally he ended up as a shopkeeper, but many people came to him because he seemed to understand something. During business hours he was a shopkeeper and the rest of the time he was a great Sufi Master.

When you jump in the river you can't plan that the fisherman will be there. It doesn't work like that. Surrender just needs tremendous trust because your mind will always come and say, 'Wait a minute! It's a very deep, fast-flowing river and my swimming is not so good.' The mind will always do that. So you can't 'do' surrender. One way to Truth is to jump into the river. The fisherman is always going to be there, but you can't make a deal with existence.

When we started our community last year we actually had no plan. The farmer invited us for a few days and then we invited ourselves for a few more days and he said okay. Then everybody was having such a nice time that I went to the farmer and said, 'Well, what do you think? What if a few people would like to live here?' He said that would be okay. So then we called a meeting. There were about forty or fifty people and I said to them, 'Look, the farmer is inviting us to make a community here and we don't have any idea. If you are interested in Awakening and you'd like to live here, then sit on that chair and tell us when you can come and what your interest is.' And twenty-five people said they would like to come.

In fact some of them disappeared and we ended up with sixteen people and we still have no plan, except we are interested in Waking Up. This needs really crazy people. To decide to leave your apartment, leave your job, sometimes leave your family and come and live in this kind of community is a bit like jumping into the river. Of course, I am not suggesting you have to come and live in our particular community to jump in the river.

We had a wonderful happening at our community recently. Lakshmi was pregnant and she's had some trouble with the pregnancy so she had been in hospital for two months. Finally the doctors decided everything was okay and they sent her home. She had been back a couple of weeks and nothing had happened and on April Fool's Day the doctor said, 'Oh, there is no sign of this baby coming for at least two weeks.' I remember passing her about eleven o'clock in the evening and I asked her, 'Well, how is it going?' And she said, 'The doctor told me today it will be at least two weeks.' We had plans to make this a big performance in the community.

Anyway, I went to sleep and it seemed like only a few minutes later somebody was waking me up, telling me that the head was already out! It had only taken an hour. This baby was there on the living room couch. One of the friends visiting the community was a midwife. She just happened to be there, and the official midwife also came quite quickly.

The hospital had sent an emergency team. They were all done up in special outfits ready for a big emergency with gas bottles and all kinds of equipment, and this little baby just popped out. It all seemed very natural to me. The emergency team sat around waiting for the emergency. There wasn't going to be one. Finally a bit desperately they said, 'Can we take you to the hospital for a check-up?' But actually everything was fine because it's always fine. While we're so busy doing our lives, it's just happening.

Question:
You told the story about jumping into the river and I asked myself: how do you get to the Source?

You are the Source. There's nowhere to get. Right now you are absolutely the Source. You are not in the Source, you are the Source. Maybe, even right now, you have some kind of illusion playing in your head telling you, 'I have to work a bit harder, I have to go to more meetings like this, maybe I need a spiritual practice, I need to read a few more books and I need to find a really good teacher and some time in the future I might get to the Source.' But you are the Source. If you would just stop, and do nothing, you would see it. If you absolutely surrender to this moment you can't avoid realising that you are the Source, right now, here, in this moment. You see the illusion of this movie that plays, and realise 'that's not me'.

I realise that I fight a lot. I have always done it and I still do it. My question is how is it possible to be a piece of wood in the water?

When you go downstairs after this meeting you might have an idea that you are going to turn left. Wait and see which way you turn, left, right or just straight across the street. Does it matter? If your car is parked on the right, one part of your mind will say, 'The quickest way is to turn right,' and the other part will say, 'Well, I want to turn left,' and then you've got a fight, a conflict. But it's all happening in your mind, in nobody else's mind, and nobody else cares. But you care. For you it is a very important decision, and therefore the fight. 'I've got to make the right choice.' But it doesn't matter, we live on a sphere!

Is your life about going the quickest way to your car, or is your life about finding Peace? It's very interesting because almost everybody in this kind of meeting would be very willing to do some really tough practice. If I said, 'Okay, if you really want Peace, then for three months or three years, or even thirty years, you have to get up at five-thirty in the morning, take a cold shower and sit in meditation for two hours, then you will find Peace.' You would say, 'Great! Okay. He's a really tough teacher, but I'll do it.' But if I say you don't have to do anything and that actually it's available right now, then what?

Last time I was in Leipzig I met a professor of Indian studies. She told me a very sad story. Twenty years ago she became very interested in enlightenment. She decided to become a professor of Indian studies so that she could really come deeply into this search for enlightenment. She studied Sanskrit so she could read all the ancient texts and she visited India several times. She told me very sadly that after twenty years she had never met this Stillness or Peace. I said, 'No problem. If you can make a little time tomorrow morning I should be able to show it to you very easily.' She said, 'Well, you know I'm very busy, I'm a professor, I have a lot of appointments.' I said, 'Come on. This is your life's desire. I'm not kidding you, come tomorrow morning and almost certainly I will be able to show you this.' So anyway, she cancelled her appointments and came to a meeting with me.

I remember we sat together in an almost empty room and I simply guided her for maybe twenty minutes from her mind, from this drama, to Stillness, which is her True Nature. It took hardly any time at all and she was really touched. She just sat there absolutely quiet, with tears running down her cheeks, and then her mobile phone rang. This was very interesting because immediately she said, 'Oh, I'm really sorry that my mobile phone has rung.' I didn't care at all, because what does it matter? Let the telephone ring. Ringing telephone, not ringing telephone, doesn't make any difference to Stillness. Immediately she said that, her mind started again. She lost touch with that Stillness.

I can't imagine that this can be a constant state. With me it's only moments.

What you are calling a constant state is your True Nature. You don't have to imagine it. You can't imagine it, but if you have some moments of Stillness you can say, 'Okay, I have "my life" and I have a few moments of Stillness. These are an experience of my True Nature.' Another way you can look at it is, 'I have my True Nature, but most of the time I have an experience of "my life".' If you have some moments, just let those moments become more. However you come there to those moments just be with that and see that all the rest, what you call 'my life', is an experience. It's not you. When this understanding becomes really clear then it is possible to live in that Stillness most of the time.

Recently, after the Arunachala Retreat, I was on the beach in India. It was very warm, sand everywhere, blue sea, wonderful sunsets and I was in a little hut right on the edge of all this paradise. The constant sound of the ocean, a little fishing village. Perfect. But then I had to come back to Germany in the middle of winter, which wasn't what Premananda wanted. I ended up in Frankfurt airport and I had my luggage on one of those trolleys. It's a very big airport and I discovered that you can push your trolley up and down the escalators. I had been in India for three months so I had great fun in the electronic shops, bookshops and the whole atmosphere of this technological masterpiece. It couldn't be any further away from the little fishing village. It was wonderful fun.

But I wasn't any different. When I got home there was snow everywhere, even on the trees. No sand, but now it was all snow. No heat, really cold. But I was still just the same. I don't depend on the temperature. I'm always the same.

Is there anybody who thinks they came to the wrong meeting? (Laughter) You might have a question. Didn't I meet you the first time I came to Leipzig?

Yes. I discovered that indifference can be a nice word.

What do you mean by indifference?

In German you can make a play with this word. It means that both have the same value.

So you've dropped judgement?

Yes.

That's good but can you see that it doesn't really make any difference? You can see the effect of this understanding on your face. Your face is really different. There's this story about a young man. He was living in a small village and one night he came home with a beautiful white horse. All the village people came and said, 'Wow! You are so lucky to find this beautiful white horse.' The next day he went for a ride on his beautiful white horse and he fell off and broke his leg. Then all the people came and said, 'Oh, what a terrible thing to happen. It wasn't so lucky to find this horse.' Then the next day the army came to the village recruiting young men. When they saw this particular young man, with a broken leg, naturally they didn't take him and then all the village people came, 'Wow! Isn't it lucky that you broke your leg and you didn't get taken by the army?' The story goes on and on.

When you really understand this it's easy just to accept what is. You can't know the future. We're constantly making these judgements: this is good, this is not good, but we can't really know it. This is just part of our illusion, just part of doing 'my life'. You can spend your whole life in that: I like this, I don't like that, he's beautiful, he's not beautiful. There's no end to it.

If you come to see this, then naturally something will relax. If I don't have money, I have more time. If I have more money, maybe I have less time. It just goes on and on, and so the invitation is to accept what is and drop the idea that I'm doing my life, that 'I know'.

Then your life has an easy flow. 'You' has melted away and the daily life, which had many problems, suddenly has a different atmosphere and you notice that things just seem to happen. They feel right, with no particular goal. Life is seen as an unfolding from moment to moment. You become aware that you are identifying with something that never changes, that just is. It has the qualities of peacefulness and silence, a deep stillness, great wellness, the sense of being surrounded by a huge warm blanket, protected and nurtured. We could call this Authentic Love and we realise that this is not something separate but is exactly our essence. We realise that in fact we are this Authentic Love and it was always so. The world changes constantly, our actions and experiences also change but at our core there is something that never changes.

Glossary

Advaita Vedanta:	One of the three systems of *Vedanta* (philosophical interpretation of the Vedas), which emphasises the strict non-duality of all. That is, everything – subjective and objective – is nothing but the Self, and the Self is paradoxically of a perfectly transcendent nature untouched by anything that appears.
Atman:	The Self.
Bhakti:	Devotion, love. Traditionally, one of the four principal approaches to God Realisation.
Chakra:	One of seven subtle spiritual centres in the body, which are located in a line from the perineum to the crown of the head. In the yogic traditions, it is said that as the *kundalini* rises, it awakens each centre progressively, giving rise to the ecstatic and visionary qualities each centre possesses.
Enneagram:	A geometric figure of ancient origin representing nine character fixations. Gurdjieff used the figure in his teachings as a symbol that represents fundamental universal cosmic laws.
Jnana:	Knowledge. Discrimination of what is real from what is not real. A principal, traditional path to realisation of the final Reality, the Self. Also the state of Realisation itself.
Jnani:	One who has realised the Self.
Leela:	Play or sport of the Divine. Philosophically, *leela* is used to explain the origin of the conditional world as arising from the humorous play of the Self.

Mala:	A circle of prayer beads like a rosary, often used as an aid for repetition of a *mantra*. The practitioner repeats the *mantra* each time he or she touches a bead. Usually contains 108 beads, of which one is different and shows the practitioner that one cycle of the *mala* has been completed.
Mantra:	Tool for the mind. Sacred sound. In the Hindu traditions, a sound from the Vedas. In the Tibetan traditions usually the name of a Tibetan deity. A *mantra* is repeated either orally or mentally and used as an aid in concentrating the mind.
Namaste:	Traditional palms-together greeting, with a slight bow at the waist. This greeting is common in social encounters in India, and strictly adhered to when greeting the guru.
Samadhi:	State of absorption in consciousness or bliss, often with little or no feeling of the ego or conventional self. Usually with eyes closed during meditation.
Sangha:	The community or gathering of devotees around a guru.
Sannyasin: (Osho Sannyasin)	Renunciate in the Osho tradition, who is given a name, a mala with a picture of Osho to wear around the neck, and is instructed to wear red clothes. A renunciate not in the traditional sense of abandoning ties with society and living an ascetic life, but rather in the sense of abandoning that which is not real or is born of the ego.
Satsang:	Abiding in the Truth. The gathering of the guru with his students.
Self-enquiry:	An ancient practice to bring the mind from the world outside back inside to the source, the Self. In recent times it has been associated with Sri Ramana Maharshi.
Vasanas:	Emotional and mental tendencies – habits of action, reaction and desire – of the persona or conditional being, which are said to be the product of patterns of living in both this life and past lives.

186

ARUNACHALA
PILGRIMAGE RETREAT

This Satsang Retreat is an opportunity to live in a community situation for three weeks at the holy mountain Arunachala in Tiruvannamalai, South India. Arunachala has been a powerful place for Self-enquiry for two thousand years. We are accommodated in a lovely modern ashram. Our meetings take place on the roof directly overlooking the holy mountain. Each morning there is quiet meditation, yoga and Satsang. We spend the afternoons alone, together with the group, or in Ramana Maharshi's ashram. Also, we go on a magical five day bus trip of 1500 km that brings us to five wonderful Indian Saints and allows us to see and experience Indian culture and landscapes.

www.india.premanandasatsang.org

Who am I?

open sky house
Be As You Are

The Open Sky House Satsang and Arts Community is housed in a seventeenth century mansion on the banks of the Rhine between Cologne and Dusseldorf, in a small village. There is a regular weekly Satsang and Energy Darshan with Premananda. In addition, regular weekend intensives and retreats are held throughout the year. There is an Arts programme consisting of painting, music, theatre and dance.

The residents work together running several businesses within the house: Open Sky Press, Rhine River Guest House, Flow Fine Art Gallery and Open Sky Seminars. All aspects of work as well as the ordinary daily life of the community like cooking, childcare, cleaning and personal communication, are used as the background to show the robotic nature of most actions. When there is freedom from habitual reactions and patterns, the mind becomes still.

You are welcome to visit as a Guest or a Volunteer.

www.openskyhouse.org

Be As You Are

Unconditional Love

Premananda

Open Sky House

Rheinstr. 54

51371 Hitdorf am Rhein

(between Cologne & Dusseldorf)

Germany

Tel: +49 2173 4099204

Mobile: +49 178 4413704

office@premanandasatsang.org

www.premanandasatsang.org